PIÆ CANTIONES

British Museum, Royal MS. 7 B. viii, f. 3b.   French (?), late xv century.

PIÆ CANTIONES

A Collection of Church & School Song,
chiefly *Ancient Swedish*, originally
published in A.D. 1582 by
THEODORIC PETRI
of *Nyland*

Revised and re-edited, with Preface
and Explanatory Notes, by the
REV. G. R. WOODWARD, M.A.
and printed at the
Chiswick Press
for the

Plainsong & Medieval Music Society

LONDON: 44, Russell Square, W.C.

M. CM. X

CHISWICK PRESS : CHARLES WHITTINGHAM AND CO.
TOOKS COURT, CHANCERY LANE, LONDON.

PIÆ CANTIO-

NES ECCLESIA-STICÆ ET SCHOLA-STICÆ VETERUM EPISCOPO-

rum, in Inclyto Regno Sueciæ paßim vsurpatæ,
nuper studio viri cuiusdam Reuerendiß: de Ecclesia
Dei & Schola Aböensi in Finlandia optime
meriti accuratè à mendis corre-
ctæ, & nunc typis com-
missæ, opera

THEODORICI PETRI
Nylandensis.

His adiecti sunt aliquot ex Psalmis recentioribus.

Imprimebatur Gryphisualdiæ,
per Augustinum Ferberum.

CANTIONES

DEDICATED

TO

HIS MAJESTY GUSTAF THE FIFTH

KING OF SWEDEN, OF THE

GOTHS AND THE

WENDS, K.G.

Preface

❡ THE present work is a new edition rather than a reprint of Theodoricus Petri's PIÆ CANTIONES (1582). Had the Committee of the Plainsong and Medieval Music Society thought fit, the original volume might have been easily reproduced in *facsimile*. Doubtless such a course would have satisfied musicians, scholars, and antiquaries. But, if the book was to be of any practical use, and possible 'in Quires and Places where they sing,' it was necessary that the old work should appear in a new shape (*aliusque et idem*). If slightly modified in the present edition, as regards some of the words, Petri's original has received the gentle handling due to a work so venerable of age, so full of piety, poetry, and musical beauty. ❡ The reasons for printing the book in its present shape rather than for reproducing it exactly as it stands are threefold: (i) The difficulty and uncertainty as to the proper distribution of the music-notes, the grouping of the musical phrases, and the lack of guidance in the determining of the slurs and ligatures. Augustin Ferber and his compositors of 1582 had been careless in the matter of registering and ranging the words beneath the notes. Therefore had this book been an exact replica of the earlier edition, the objection would have been perpetuated, not removed. As it is, an attempt has been made, occasionally more by guesswork than with absolute certainty, to print the Latin words exactly below their

proper

proper notes. (ii) It was felt that the great variety of clefs (no fewer than nine) employed in the original work might prove an obstacle in some quarters; though, with a little patience and practice, the old clefs become easy as A B C, especially when only one occasional B moll is introduced into the signature, and all sharps are excluded. But, as a concession to the weaker brethren, and to encourage and facilitate the use of this book, the bulk of the tunes have been transposed into the ordinary treble and bass (or barytone) clefs. At the same time, beyond transposition, no liberty whatsoever has in any case been taken with the musical value or with the position of any note of the music. The ancient sixteenth century notation has been retained, as being more artistic than the modern style of the twentieth century founts, and as being more in keeping with an old-fashioned music-book, such as this is. (iii) But the principal hindrance in the way of printing these PIÆ CANTIONES, as a whole, was their introduction and toleration of certain grave doctrinal errors. Petri himself, or the Very Rev. gentleman of Åbo, of whom he speaks in his title-page, had submitted some of the excellent work of the *Veteres Episcopi* to severe treatment; chiefly in regard to certain expressions of their devotion to her whom all generations shall call Blessed. He should have left their writings alone. *Certe piè interpretanda, quæ tantæ pietatis imaginem præ se ferunt.* Loth to lose altogether some of the choicest gems of the Old Church *Carmina Mariana*, Petri, being one of the 'New Religion,' felt constrained to transform some of the *Cantiones* in honour of Our Lady into *Cantiones* in worship of Our Lord. Consequently, in order to make these pre-Reformation Canticles fall into line with the received Lutheran notions of Orthodoxy, Petri allowed them deliberately to be altered, not for

the

the better but for the worfe. One might overlook the
bad tafte of thefe Renaiffance theologians in ftyling Our
Lord the *Son of Lucrece*;[1] one might forgive the faulty
rimes and affonances[2] which thefe clumfy hymn-menders
fubftituted for the fine workmanfhip of the Old Church
medieval clerks and cloifter-men; but it was impoffible
in this new edition of 1909 to repeat and ftereotype the
ftrange blunders and meaninglefs fimiles, which were
the inevitable confequences of this unneceffary and non-
theological tampering with the old text. It was one
thing to call the Bleffed Virgin another Judith, a fecond
Jael, a new Efther, but quite another matter to apply
thefe terms to Our Lord. Then it became nonfenfe.
It was well enough to compare the Mother of God to
the Ark that bare the true Mofes of His People; the
Veffel containing the very Manna from heaven; the
Throne of Solomon; and to defcribe her as ' Porta claufa
nec peruia,' but abfurd to transfer thefe figures to Our
Lord. But far worfe. Like the men in the Pfalms,
' brought into great fear where no fear was,' Petri and his
Lutheran advifers, wifhing to avoid all appearance of
Mariolatry, fell unintentionally into the other extreme,
and became guilty of herefy concerning the divinity of
Mary's Son and Mary's Saviour. So it happened to them
according to the true proverbs: *Incidis in Scyllam cupiens
vitare Charybdim*;[3] and again, *Dum vitant ftulti vitia, in
contraria currunt*.[4] The phrafe, 'Te decet *poft Dominum*
laus honor et poteftas'[5] was all right when applied to
Bleffèd Mary, but all wrong when transferred to Our

[1] Lúcretïæ natus (fee No. XXXIX, p. 67, l. 3).
[2] Virgo fine viro peperit te,
Et poft virginem declarauit fe (No. XXIV, pp. 36 and 239).
[3] Philippe Gaultier, 'Alexandreis,' bk. v, l. 301, *circa* 1300.
[4] Horace, Sat. i, 2, 24.
[5] See *Cantio* (No. XXVI, p. 42, l. 1).

Lord

Lord. To say 'O Virgo, filia Patris qui te fecerat' was perfectly correct; but to parody the words, and say 'Dei Nate, Fili grate Patris, qui te fecerat'[1] was utterly incorrect, and at variance with the Nicene statement that Our Lord was begotten, not made (*genitum non factum*). Consequently there was no alternative but to restore these particular *Cantiones* to their original integrity, and with the assistance of Dreves and Blume's 'Analecta Hymnica' this duty has been done as faithfully as possible.

❡ A few words concerning the SVPPLEMENTVM (pp. 91-201). Although each of Petri's PIÆ CANTIONES possesses an interest of its own, it was not to be expected, in a collection of seventy-three, that all should be of equal merit. Some were bound to be less tuneful, or more difficult and lengthy than their fellows; and it was felt that the introduction of these less desirable numbers would increase the size and cost of the book, and therefore their room was thought more welcome than their company. In some cases, too, there were unusual difficulties in fitting the text to the tune, and in other instances it was foreseen that some of the *Cantiones* were not likely to win much popularity. Consequently, at the outset, the Plainsong and Medieval Music Society decided to make a selection of the likeliest. But who should choose between the wheat and the chaff? Fifty-two undoubtedly of the best were already set up in type, and printed off, and a complete list of all the omissions was ready for the press, with the first lines of the words, and the *Sic incipit* of the various tunes, and parts of the tunes, when, in accordance with the advice of competent judges, the Society reconsidered their decision, and finally determined to reprint the whole collection.

[1] See *Cantio* No. LXX, p. 26c, St. 11, l. 5.

Otherwise

Otherwife many interefting lyrics, many quaint and flowing melodies, and feveral early fpecimens of polyphonic mufic-writing would have been excluded. This refiduum of exactly fix and twenty has therefore been printed in the SVPPLEMENTVM; wherein, unlike the previous part of the book, the ancient clefs have been fyftematically preferved, and the tunes reproduced as they ftand in PIÆ CANTIONES.[1] Where the plainfong, or tenor only, of a fetting had been already given in the body of the book, it has been repeated in the Supplement, with the addition of the defcant, alto, and bafs, if any. ❡ At firft it was propofed to iffue the fifty-two, without preface or commentary, and to let them fpeak for themfelves; but later on, it feemed better to write a preface and notes. It is to be regretted that Petri of Nyland in 1582 left nothing on record, beyond the fcant information contained in his title-page, as to the fources, origin, hiftory, and nationality of his words and tunes. Had he only foreknown the appreciation in ftore for his literary and mufical efforts he would affuredly have remedied this omiffion, and thus made his book even more valuable than it is. ❡ For the following particulars of Petri's family hiftory and life we are indebted to Tobias Norlind.[2] Theodoric Petri belonged to an ariftocratic Finnifh family. His grandfather, Jöns Jute, had migrated from Denmark to Finland in the beginning of the fixteenth century. His father, Peder Jönffon, had been ennobled, and had become the poffeffor of landed property in Borgå. Didrik (Theodoric) was the youngeft fon. Early in the year 1580 this Didrik, with his elder brother Johannes, left Åbo in Finland, and went to Roftock (about eighty miles north-eaft of Lübeck) to ftudy at the Univerfity, founded there in 1418. In

[1] All, except three. [2] 'Svenfk Mufik hiftoria,' pp. 49-51, Lund. 1901.

1582, while a student, he edited a collection of Church and School Songs entitled Piæ Cantiones. In the following year he published in elegiac verse an ode in memory of his brother's departure from Roftock. In Hamburg in 1589 there followed a Latin poem on the death of one Henrik Ranzovij. In 1591 he was appointed secretary to King Sigifmund. He was alive in 1625, for in that year he superintended the publication of a new and somewhat enlarged edition of his Piæ Cantiones. The latter part of his life was spent in Poland, where also he died. Yet a third edition in Latin had to be provided during the second half of the seventeenth century. These Piæ Cantiones spread over the whole of Finland and Sweden. In 1616 Rector H. Hemming, of Mafku, caused an edition to be printed in the vernacular. In 1619 Haakon Laurentij à Rhezelio included many of Petri's Piæ Cantiones tunes in his 'Någre Pfalmer,'[1] a collection of pfalms and hymns in the Swedish tongue. In Swedish schools they survived until 1700. In Finland, in 1761, a selection of them was made by Joh. Lindell, but without music. On page 16 of his 'Svenfk Mufik historia,' 1901, Tobias Norlind informs us that some of the Piæ Cantiones continued to be sung as Christmas and Easter carols—sung and danced by school-children—until late in the nineteenth century at Björneborgs in Finland. *Ave maris ftella, divinitatis cella* was an especial favourite. So, too, among school songs, was *O fcholares voce pares*. On page 104 he again assures us that Piæ Cantiones has always held the first rank, and in various places he bears testimony to 'the richnefs of its contents,' to its 'popularity with young students,' to its 'freshnefs and naturalnefs,' to its 'superiority over the German song-books for schools.'

---

[1] A copy of this work is in the British Mufeum.

Piæ

¶ PIÆ CANTIONES, in its original vellum binding, is a small octavo volume, measuring 5¾ by 3¾ inches.

TENOR.

It consists of ninety-nine folios (*recto* and *verso*) and is printed throughout in italic, presumably in pica or small

pica

pica type. The music is written above the words of the
first stanza, in the notation of the period, generally five
scores to the page, and is, of course, unbarred, except
the final double bars at the close. It is interesting if only
because it is the first example of a Swedish book printed
in measured music.[1]

❡ The task that Petri set before himself was to
rescue and preserve for future use some of the most
beautiful psalms, hymns, and school songs of the Medieval Church in Finland.[2] When he calls his book, PIÆ
CANTIONES, the work of Bishops of the Old unreformed
Church, it must be remembered that the term Bishop
would include Priests as well, and such as had the oversight and charge of souls.[3] He speaks of the *Cantiones*
as being in vogue throughout Sweden, but they had
been recently revised through the industry of a certain
Very Rev. gentleman who had rendered great service to
the Church of God and to the School at Åbo in Finland.
They were now edited by himself, Theodoric Petri,
of the province of Nyland, a Swede, or, more accurately,
a Finlander.[4] The collection, supplemented by several
hymns of more recent date, was published at Greisswald
(not far from Rostock) in Western Pomerania, then
part of Sweden, but afterwards in 1815 annexed by
Prussia. It was printed at Augustin Ferber's office, and
the colophon supplies the date, 1582.

❡ Petri dedicates the book to his Mæcenas, The

[1] T. Norlind, p. 43.

[2] In Petri's days, and long after, down to 1809, Finland formed
part of the kingdom of Sweden.

[3] See Du Cange's 'Glossarium ad Script. mediæ et infimæ
Latinitatis,' tom. iii, f. 107; also H. P. Liddon's 'Explanatory
Analysis of St. Paul's First Epistle to Timothy' (1907), p. 21.

[4] Later on called Ruutas, *i.e.*, of Ruuta, from the name of his
home. See T. Norlind, p. 15.

Noble

Noble and Illustrious Christian Horn (son of Nicolas) Free Baron of Aminna.[1]

❡ Here is a brief analysis of Petri's preface. Petri is well aware of the value and effect of music, vocal and instrumental, in stirring up the wills, and in ordering and raising the affections of mankind. This was the teaching of the Fathers and Prophets, such as David, Nathan, and Gad in the Old Testament, and this the advice of St. Paul to the Colossians and Ephesians in the New. This was fully recognized by the wise rulers and devout bishops of bygone generations, many of whom were to be found in his beloved country; men who employed music, no less than the other arts, for the worship of God. Even in the dark ages, when the Gospel light was obscured by sundry sophistries, superstitions, and idolatrous customs God raised up many godly persons who worshipped him aright. Witness this book of spiritual songs. Careless scribes and unskilful clerks are apt to make mistakes in copying old manuscripts. Hence certain errors had crept into the text of his *Cantiones*, but these have been corrected. These *Cantiones* are more like rhythmical verse than poetry. Often there occur traces of the old Latinity once in use in monasteries and schools. But these are of such a character that, on account of their old-world religious feeling, they seem to deserve our veneration, with frank allowance for their extreme age, rather than to merit the ridicule and gainsaying of the scornful. The reader and admirer of Vergil and Horace has no need, on that account, to despise the works of old Ennius and Lucretius. ❡ As for the *Cantiones* for two, three, or four voices, because

[1] The 'Sveriges Ridderskaps och Adel Kalender,' Stockholm, 1908, mentions the fact that this ancient Swedo-Finnish family, Horn of Aminna, baroneted in 1561, is still in existence.

they differed in no small degree from the then existing rules of music, Petri says that he has entrusted them to the care of a certain person highly commended for his knowledge and experience both in the theory and in the practice of music, to be examined and brought into conformity with the rules of later musicians; so that, when published, they cannot fail to meet with the approbation even of the greatest adepts in that art. ⁋ Finally, in the belief that these *Cantiones* will be of some profit to the Church and schools of his beloved fatherland, he feels it his bounden duty to put forth this book, which he has caused to be printed in elegant type. With some grateful and respectful remarks concerning his patron, he dates his preface from Rostock, 23rd May, 1582. After the preface are printed six couplets of elegiac verse, founded on Isaiah iv, 9 & 11, in honour of Our Lord's Nativity, beginning *Nascere Iusticiæ, promissum nascere semen*, composed by one Henricus Husanus, Iuris Consultus, but they are nothing remarkable.

⁋ The particular copy of Piæ Cantiones used for this work was brought into England by Mr. G. J. R. Gordon,[1] not later than the beginning of 1853. It is believed that he gave the precious volume to his friend, the Rev. John Mason Neale.[2] The latter in turn

[1] H. M. Queen Victoria's Envoy and Minister at Stockholm, and later on at Bern and Hanover; an occasional contributor of articles on Swedish churches, etc., in 'The Ecclesiologist,' between the years 1853-63.

[2] Neale, with his admirable judgement and naturally musical ear, thoroughly appreciated the beauty of the words and melodies of Piæ Cantiones. In 1853-4 he and the Rev. T. Helmore published their 'Carols for Christmas and Easter-tide.' In free imitation rather than in close translation of the original, Neale wrote four and twenty carols to suit the metre and the melodies

handed

handed it on to his friend, the Rev. Thomas Helmore, who bequeathed it to his son, Mr. Arthur Helmore, from whom it was purchased in 1908 by the Plain Song and Medieval Music Society, in London. Amongst its owners, previous to 1853, as it tells us itself, may be mentioned the names of Eric Linning (?), Eric Linderstedt, and Pehr Frigel[1] (1750-1842). The book is now exceedingly rare, if not quite unique. It is not to be found in the British Museum, nor have the Editors of 'Analecta Hymnica,' in the course of their wanderings and researches in the principal libraries of Europe, so far discovered a duplicate. In vol. xlv*b* of the aforesaid collection are to be found many of the contents of PIÆ CANTIONES, but it may be assumed that these are taken second-hand from Herr Gustaf Edvard Klemming's[2] reprint of Petri's work. Herr Klemming may

of some of these ancient Songs. Of these carols no less an authority than Mr. W. S. Rockstro makes the following remarks in his article, under the heading of 'Noël,' in Grove's 'Dict. of Music' (1880), vol. ii, p. 463: 'The best, as well as the most popular English Carols of the present day are translations from well-known medieval originals. The Rev. J. M. Neale has been peculiarly happy in his adaptations, among which are the long-established favourites "Christ was born on Christmas-day" (*Resonet in laudibus*); "Good Christian men, rejoice and sing" (*In dulci iubilo*); "Royal day that chasest gloom" (*Dies est laeticiae*); and "Good King Wenceslas look'd out" (*Tempus adest floridum*) . . . a work which, notwithstanding its modest pretensions, is by far the best collection published in a popular form.'

[1] An eminent Swedish composer. See T. Norlind, p. 163, and R. Eitner's 'Quellen-Lexikon,' Bd. iv, p. 85.

[2] See G. E. Klemming's 'Hymni, Sequentiæ et Piæ Cantiones' (1886), and his 'Cantiones Morales, Scholasticæ, Historicæ in regno Sueciæ olim usurpatæ' (1887). Klemming has enriched his books with many other similar sacred songs, and he mentions the various libraries and monasteries in such places as Åbo, Upsala, Wadstena, Stockholm, Skara, Strengnås and Linköping, with the names of

however

however have had access to some copy of Piæ Cantiones
other than that which is now in England. But as he
was acquainted with Mr. G. J. R. Gordon, and in
correspondence with the Rev. J. M. Neale,[1] it seems
more probable that he made use of this particular copy.
The rarity of Piæ Cantiones receives further proof
from the significant silence of Meister and Bäumker
(both of them Roman Catholicks) who have compiled
three vols. of ancient melodies, but have taken no notice

the old MSS. and printed graduals, antiphoners, missals, tropers,
hymners, and psalters which he has laid under contribution for
his interesting and choice collection. T. Norlind also names the
chief places in Sweden and Finland where are to be found the
writings of some of the *Veteres Episcopi*, which Petri may perhaps
have incorporated in his book. He also records (on pages 9 and
10) the names of some of the early church singers of Sweden,
among whom are Henrik, Bishop of Linköping (1272); Nils
Allesson, Abp. of Upsala (1298); Brynolphus I, Bishop of Skara
(1317); and amongst 'Cloister Singers' in Sweden he mentions Magister Petrus, Kætilmund (1384), Christina Niclasdotter
(1399), and Margareta Lassadotter (1402), these last being apparently nuns in St. Bridget's Convent at Wadstena.

[1] Thanks to the courtesy of this learned Herr Klemming, Neale
was enabled to include in the various numbers of 'The Ecclesiologist' (referred to by Daniel, Kehrein, and Chevalier) several
sequences occurring in certain early printed Swedish missals.
Amongst these are ' Audi, virgo, mater Christi,' ' Celi chorus esto
gaudens,' ' Felix vixit hic Confessor,' etc. And yet these sequences,
with about eighty others published in 'The Ecclesiologist' between the years 1853-63, *i.e.*, about half a century ago (more or
less), now appear, as though for the first time, labelled Seqventiæ
Ineditæ, in ' Analecta Hymnica ' (1886-1907). See vols. viii, ix,
x, xxxiv, xxxvii, xxxix, xl, xlii, and xliv. This is not intended to
depreciate the value of Messrs. Dreves and Blume's exhaustive
work, but it is only justice to the memory and name of our fellow
countryman, John Mason Neale, one of the greatest pioneers of
Europe in the study of hymnology, to record this fact. Honour
to whom honour is due!

of

of this important book. Carl von Winterfeld and Joh.
Zahn (both Lutherans) were evidently alſo in ignorance
of its exiſtence, although in his admirable ſix vols.
entitled 'Die Melodien der deutſcher Evangeliſchen
Kirchenlieder' the latter quotes ſeveral tunes taken
from two editions of 'Ein new Chriſtlich Pſalmbuch,'
printed alſo at Greifswald, and that, too, on Auguſtin
Ferber's printing-preſs, in 1592 and 1597 reſpectively,
i.e., only ten and fifteen years after Petri's publication.
F. M. Böhme in his 'Alt Deutſcher Liederbuch,' p. 781,
ſpeaks of a 'Greifswalder Geſangbuch' of 1592, containing eighty melodies, alſo printed by Ferber. But
never a word about Piæ Cantiones, 1582.

℃ In the preface to his 'Carols for Chriſtmas-Tide'
(1853) Neale obſerves that 'It is impoſſible at one ſtretch
to produce a quantity of New Carols, of which words
and muſic alike ſhall be original. They muſt be the
gradual accumulation of centuries; the offerings of
different epochs, of different countries, of different
minds, to the ſame treaſury of the Church. None but
an empiric would venture to make a ſet to order.'
Petri of Nyland has proved the truth of this aſſertion.
For his Piæ Cantiones range from the tenth to the
latter part of the ſixteenth century, and they are the
product of various countries, the compoſition of many
minds. Thus, if the greater part be of Swedo-Finniſh
origin, many are to be found in ancient German pre-Reformation hymn-books, but perhaps the oldeſt of all may
prove to be a native of Southern Europe, *Congaudeat* (or
En gaudeat) *turba fidelium*, for it is contained in a French
book of the tenth century. A certain number come
from Bohemia and Moravia, and are of Huſſite parentage. As for thoſe *ex Pſalmis recentioribus*, Petri naturally
made uſe of ſome of the Lutheran ſong books. For

two

two at leaſt he is indebted to Lucas Loſſius, Lutheran, of Lüneberg, author of 'Pſalmodia Sacra' (1553-79). There is a ſtriking ſimilarity between the preface of theſe two editors, Loſſius and Petri. Each has his Maecenas; indeed Loſſius can boaſt of a couple of royal patrons. Even the title of Petri's book[1] ſeems to have been ſuggeſted by Loſſius, when the latter ſpeaks of the Pɪᴀᴇ Cᴀɴᴛɪᴏɴᴇs which he has drawn from various ſources. It is impoſſible at this diſtance of time to aſcertain of what collections Petri made principal uſe; but in the notes at the end of this volume, under each *Cantio*, will be given the names of the chief MSS. written, and books printed, before 1582, in which Petri's words and tunes, with variations great or ſmall, are to be ſeen. There is no trace of any Calviniſtic influence in Petri's book. It may be ſtated that ſeveral well-known contemporary *Cantiones*, ſuch as *Quem paſtores laudauere, Nunc Angelorum gloria, In natali Domini, Surrexit Chriſtus hodie, Patris sapiencia, Ave hierarchia*, are conſpicuous by their abſence, and it is hard to underſtand on what principle ſome were taken and others left.

❡ Concerning the authors of the words and tunes contained in Pɪᴀᴇ Cᴀɴᴛɪᴏɴᴇs. They are for the moſt part unknown. No doubt they have been forgotten, partly through the ingratitude of ſucceeding generations; partly, and more probably, becauſe theſe compoſers who 'found out muſical tunes and recited verſes in writing,' ſo far from writing for filthy lucre or for

---

[1] 'Pſalmodia—hoc eſt Cantica Sacra veteris Eccleſiæ . . . Ad eccleſiarum et Scholarum uſum olim diligenter collecta . . . nunc autem recens accurata diligentia et fide recognita, et multis utilibus ac *pijs cantionibus* aucta per Lucam Loſſium, Luneburgenſem, 1569.'

fame's

fame's sake, so far from seeking notoriety, rather shunned
it. Many a church poet and musician was content,
from motives of humility, that his name should be con-
cealed. Nevertheless, in some few cases, the names, if
nothing more, of the authors have been discovered and
preserved. For instance *Iesus Christus nostra salus* is
undoubtedly the workmanship of Johannes Hus; witness the Acrostic. *In dulci iubilo* may be almost certainly ascribed to John Tauler's friend, the Dominican
Friar, Heinrich Suso; while the Acrostics RAGVVALDVS,
OLAVVS, BIRCERVS, JOHANNES, THOMAS FECIT, leave
no doubt as to the Christian name, if nothing else, of their
several writers.

❡ The contents of the book (1582) consist of Seventy-
four items,[1] and come under eleven groups: (I) Four
and twenty *Cantiones* for Christmas-tide (many of which
were originally in honour of Our Lady); (II) Nine
for Passion-tide and Easter; (III) One for Pentecost;
(IV) Three for Trinity Sunday; (V) Two on the Holy
Eucharist; (VI) Four Songs of Prayer; (VII) Fourteen
of the Frailty and Miseries of this Mortal State; (VIII)
Ten on School Life; (IX) Two on Concord; (X) Three
Historical; (XI) Two on Spring-tide. ❡ As might be

[1] If the *Seventy-four* Carols, in the Old Edition, seem now to
have grown into *Seventy-eight* in the New, the apparent discrep-
ancy is to be accounted for thus: (i) *Cedit hyems eminus* figures
twice over; viz., as No. XVII (with the Tenor melody only),
and again, in the SVPPLEMENTVM, as No. LIX (with the addition of the Descant and the Bass parts); (ii) the same may be said
of *Iucundare iugiter* (which occurs as Nos. XVIII and LX);
(iii) *O dulcis Iesus*, No. LXII, has been taken out of *Laus Virginis*, No. LXVII, and printed by itself; (iv) *Magnum nomen
Domini*, No. LXXVIII, has been separated from *Resonet in laudibus*, No. III, and treated as a Carol complete in itself. Hence
74+4=78. Q. E. D.

expected

expected from the pens of the *Veteres Episcopi*, whom Petri so rightly eulogizes, these Piæ Cantiones are full of expressions of the deepest religious feeling. There is music in the very mention of the Christmas Carols *In dulci iubilo, Dies est leticie, Puer natus in Bethlehem, Omnis mundus iucundetur, Resonet in laudibus;* all of them remarkable for their store of sound theology, stated clearly, briefly, and with much naïveté. (*Summa ars celare artem.*) Many of these Finnish strains as *Laus Virginis, Vnica gratifera, Ave Maris Stella (ij)* are noteworthy for their intimate knowledge of the Bible, and for their apt and frequent application of Old Testament types to Our Lord, or to his Mother, and are re-echoes of the patristic interpretation of Holy Scripture. Some of the sequences are almost worthy of Adam of St. Victor himself. ❡ Nor are the *Cantiones* for Easter and those on the Blessed Sacrament less admirable than the carols for the Nativity of Our Lord. ❡ The *Cantiones* beginning *Vanitatum vanitas* and *Mundanis vanitatibus* sound more like the aged King Solomon's 'Vanity of vanities, all is vanity,' than the 'experience' of a Rostock Undergraduate. The candid admission in *O mentes perfidas* (if written by a Catholick) that even *Romana curia | fouet periuria* is to be noticed. No *laudator temporis acti* will find anything wherewith to disagree in Petri's unfavourable contrast betwixt the present and the past, as delineated in *Honestatis decus iam mutatur*, but will welcome his jeremiad over the decay of morals and manners, and the curse of *ebria modernitas*, apparently already at work in the sixteenth century. ❡ The songs on school-life are spirited, humorous, and merry, containing useful advice, warnings, and salutary maxims, as applicable to a Winchester, Eton, or Harrow boy in the twentieth, as to a student

at

at Åbo in Finland in the sixteenth, century. For the happiness of school days, read *O scholares voce pares.* For school boys' faults, turn to *Castitatis speculum.* If there be any lads unable to read music or to scan Latin verse, who *Vix sciunt G, Vt, A, RE | Nec MVSA declinare,* let them peruse *Scholares conuenite.* For high ideals, see *O Scholares discite, Schola morum floruit,* or *Disciplinæ filius.* Few boys will fail to appreciate such lines as these 'Felix ludus | in quo nudus | scholaris verberibus | non succumbit | nec decumbit | magistri liuoribus': or this 'Taurum domat rusticus | ictu, fuste, restibus, | puerum Scholasticus | verbis et verberibus.'

⁋ Englishmen will read with especial interest and pride the historical Cantio *Ramus virens oliuarum,* for it recounts the life and death of the English St. Henry, Priest of York, afterwards Archbishop of Upsala, the Apostle of Finland, and Martyr, A.D. 1157. ⁋ Two songs of spring-tide bring the collection (1582) to a close. ⁋ The tunes to which the words are wedded are worthy of them. ⁋ The whole book is possessed of a healthy tone, of a religious, chivalrous spirit, with an elevating civilizing influence, and is interesting if only because it sets forth the then accepted standard of all that was good, noble, and beautiful in ordinary daily life.

⁋ For reasons already given on p. x of this Preface, most of the Melodies in the earlier part of this present Work (1910) have been transposed. But in the SVPPLE-MENTVM (with the exception of Nos. LIII, LV, and LXXIII), all are reproduced in their original Clefs. The same remark applies to Nos. II, XII, XIII, and XLVIII.

⁋ Nine Clefs were employed in PIÆ CANTIONES (1582):

The

(i) The Bass Clef (F on the fourth line). This was the Clef of Nos. IV, XII, XIII, XIV, XXIX, XLVIII, and LXI.

(ii) The Barytone Clef (F on the third line). In this Clef were written Nos. I, V, X, XI, XII, XVI, XXII, XXIII, XXVIII, XXXII, XXXIII, XXXVII, XL, XLV, XLVI, XLIX, L, LVIII, LIX, LX, LXIV, LXVI, LXVII, LXXIV, LXXVI.

(iii) The Contra-tenor Clef (C on the top line). The above was employed in the following instances: Nos. XXVI, XXXV, XXXVIII, XLIII, LV, LXII, LXVI, and LXVII.

(iv) The Tenor Clef (C on the fourth line). The above claims the under-named *Cantiones*: Nos. VI, VIII, IX, XVII, XVIII, XIX, XX, XXI, XXV, XXVII, XXX, XXXI, XXXIV, XXXIX, XLI, XLIV, XLVII, LIII, LVI, LVII, LVIII, LIX, LX, LXIII, LXV, LXVIII, LXIX, LXX, LXXII, LXXIII, LXXV, and LXXVII.

(v) The Alto Clef (C on the middle line). This is the Clef of Nos. III, VII, XIV, XV, XXXV, LII, LVIII, LXI, LXXI, LXXIV, LXXVI, and LXXVIII.

(vi) The Mezzo-Soprano Clef (C on the second line). This is found in Nos. XXIV, LIX, and LX.

The

(vii) The Soprano Clef (C on the firſt
line). Nos. LI and LXI.

(viii) The Low Treble Clef (G on the
middle line). Nos. XIV and LIV.

(ix) The Treble Clef (G on the ſecond
line). Nos. II and LXXIII.

❡ In Grove's 'Dictionary of Muſic and Muſicians'
(1907), Vol. III, p. 405, Mr. W. S. Rockſtro remarks
that the Contra-Tenor Clef (No. iv) was 'very rarely
uſed after about the middle of the ſixteenth century.'
It will be noticed that Nos. vii and viii are, practically,
one and the ſame Clef.

❡ The SIMPLE NOTES employed are theſe:[1]

(a) The Long . . . . .

(b) The Breve . . . . .

[1] For full information as to the art of expreſſing muſical ideas
and muſical ſounds in writing, the ſtudent is referred to Grove's
'Dictionary of Muſic and Muſicians' (1907), Vol. III, pp. 392-407;
the article on *Notation*.

The

(*c*) The Semibreve . . . .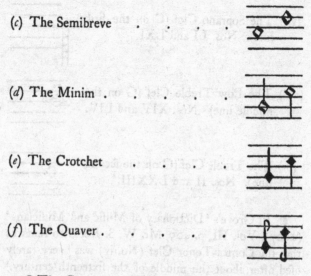

(*d*) The Minim . . . . .

(*e*) The Crotchet . . . .

(*f*) The Quaver . . . . .

¶ The Compound Notes employed are these:

(*a*) The descending 'ligature' (the relic of the Plainsong 'clivis'):

Fig. i

(*b*) The ascending 'ligature' (the relic of the Plainsong 'podatus'):

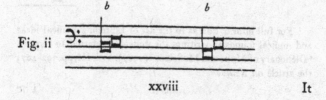

Fig. ii

It

It is moſt neceſſary to underſtand the law of the 'liga-ture,' *i.e.*, of the 'bound,' 'tied,' or 'ſlurred' double-notes. (N.B.—*In a ligature, whether aſcending or deſcending, which bears a riſing tail on its left ſide, the notes are Semi-breves.*)

Thus the notes marked *a* in Fig. i are to be reckoned, in modern muſic, ſeverally, as Semibreves:

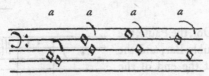

The notes marked *b* in Fig. ii are to be reckoned, in modern muſic, ſeverally, as Semibreves:

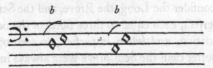

¶ As in modern muſic, 3 at the be-ginning of a ſtave ſtands for Triple or Perfect Time.

¶ The signs at *c*, *c*, ſtand for Imperfect Time. Though **C** is now conſidered to be the ſhort for Common Time, it ori-ginally ſignified that the Triple, *i.e.*, the Perfect Time (often marked with a circle, denoting perfection, as at *d*, or with a circle pierced with an upright bar as at *e*) was broken and imperfect.[1]

[1] 'Wichtig iſt die hiſtoriſche Thatſache: daſz wir bis ins 14. Jahrhundert hinein keine Spur eines Zweitheiligen Taktes finden,

The

The ♭ is ufed occafionally: the ♯, and the ♮, never.

The reft below the line fignifies the Semi-breve Reft;

The reft on the line, the Minim Reft.

Of the Dot, the Paufe, the small double Bar, and the Guide at the end of the line, nothing need be faid.

❡ In the time of PIÆ CANTIONES, 1582, the cuftom was to confider the Long, the Breve, and the Semibreve, when perfect, each equal to three notes of the next leffer denomination, and when imperfect, to two only: but notes fhorter than the Semibreve were always imperfect. Thus, in triple time, if two Breves came in fucceffion the firft * is confidered as a dotted note, and equal to

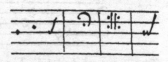

or - tu   le - ta - bun - do. (P.C. xxv.)

three Semibreves. But as a guide to the right inter-pretation of the tunes in PIÆ CANTIONES, it is to be obferved (i) that the melodies, though not hampered by bars, are ftrictly metrical, and if the value of the various

fondern blos das tempus perfectum (Tripel Takt).'—F. M. Böhme, Pref., p. liv, ' Alt deutfches Lied.'

notes employed be remembered, and if only the above important rule as to the ufe of the ligature be obferved, there need be no difficulty in reading thefe *Cantiones* at fight.

❡ No bars are employed, except at the final clofe at the end of each *Cantio.*

❡ Concerning the Metres. Piæ Cantiones gives us a pleafing variety. Here, in more fenfes than one, is no 'common meafure.' It would be poffible, but an unprofitable tafk, to analyze the metres of each of thefe facred or fecular fongs, and to call them by their technical names. Suffice it to ftate, in general, that the principal feet, of which thefe verfes are compofed, are a mixture of iambus, trochee, and fpondee. The writers, as a rule, difpenfed with the old anapæft, dactyl, and amphibrach, or left them to be adopted by later generations. Piæ Cantiones abounds in trochaic, or feminine endings, and double rimes. If not formed on the lines of the Minnefinger, or with *Stollen* and *Abgefang*, many of the *Cantiones* end with fome graceful and telling chorus or refrain. Examples of this are *Angelus emittitur, Ave Maris ftella diuinitatis cella, Ecce nouum gaudium, Difciplinæ filius, Scribere propofui.* The ftanzas range in length from two to fourteen lines. The fequences, fuch as *Pfallat fidelis concio* and *Autor humani generis* naturally alter their rhythm and metre repeatedly.

❡ Of the Harmonies. Twelve fettings in all: *Cantiones* (A) *duarum*, (B) *trium*, (C) *quattuor vocum.* There are eight two-part fettings; two arranged for three voices; and two for a quartet. They are as follows:

(A) For Two Voices.

1. *Paranymphus adiens.*
2. *Ad cantus leticie* (in *rondo* form).
3. *Puer natus in Bethlehem* (the chief melody in the bafs).

Jucundare

4. *Jucundare iugiter.*
5. *Parce Virgo (Parce Christe).*
6. *Ieremiæ prophetiæ.*
7. *Regimen scholarium.*
8. *Zachæus arboris.*

(B) For Three Voices.

9. *Ætas carmen melodiæ.*
10. *Cedit hyems eminus* (the melody in the bass, but gradually superseded by the tenor; see No. LIX).

(c) For Four Voices.

11. *Gaudete, gaudete Christus est natus.*
12. *Iesu dulcis memoria.*

¶ Of the TONALITY. In several instances it is difficult to decide whether the melodies are to be ascribed to the ancient Lydian mode, the fifth, or to the Ionian, the thirteenth, the modern major scale, commonly known as *il modo lascivo*, whose star was even then in the ascendant. But in most cases, it is easy to determine the tonality of each of the PIÆ CANTIONES. About two and twenty fulfil the requirements of the 'grave' Dorian, or first Gregorian mode. Five or six belong to the 'sedate' Hypo-dorian, *i.e.*, to the second tone. About fourteen may be attributed to the 'mystic' Phrygian third mode, or to the 'harmonious' Hypophrygian. Two or three belong to the Mixo-lydian, the seventh tone (*tonus angelicus* or *tonus iuvenum*) but apparently only one to the 'perfect' Hypo-mixo-lydian, the eighth tone (or *tonus sapientum*). ¶ Herein lies the secret of the strength, the charm, the freshness, the perpetual youth, the vitality, the indescribable beauty of these old-world airs. The great difference between this venerable music and that of a later date is to be

accounted

accounted for by the peculiarity of the scales, *i.e.*, the modes in which the various melodies were written. Whereas modern composers are commonly content with two modes only, the major and the minor, the former when they desire to be merry, and the latter when melancholy,[1] in earlier times musicians employed one or other of at least eight different scales, each being distinguished, like the major and minor of our own days, by the position of the semi-tones. These ancient scales were not limited to Church music; but many of the finest English, Scottish, Irish, Welsh, French, German, Scandinavian and other national secular melodies, folk and school songs, fulfilled the laws of these old scales or *maneria*, and derived their peculiar strength and character from the peculiar position of the tones and semi-tones in the modes to which they belong. Though the beauty of the delightful airs in PIÆ CANTIONES will be admitted on all sides, and though they are considered by competent musicians masterpieces of pure flowing melody, and wonderfully fine specimens of rhythm, nothing appears to be known concerning their composers.

❡ Several of the Melodies contained in this Collection, though not necessarily taken from it, have in bygone ages attracted the attention of many of the most eminent musicians of Europe. For instance, J. Walther, S. Calvisius, M. Prætorius, J. H. Schein, S. Scheidt, J. Crüger, D. Buxtehude, F. W. Zachau, J. Pachelbel, J. G. Walther, and last, but not least, J. S. Bach, were in their several generations fully aware of the beauty of *In dulci iubilo, Puer natus in Bethlehem, Dies est leticie, Resonet in laudibus, Iesus Christus nostra salus, Cedit*

---

[1] To prove the absurdity of this idea, be it remembered that Handel wrote his mournful 'Dead March in Saul' in the key of C major, but his merry 'O ruddier than the cherry' in G minor.

hyems eminus, etc., and have left us many exquisite settings of these Carols, treated in various ways, reverently and lovingly handled, and harmonized, for the most part, with marvellous skill. In the Explanatory Notes, at the end of this Volume, an attempt has been made to give references (though, by no means, exhaustive ones) to some of the principal Choral and Song Books, Organ and Choral-prelude Works, of the Great Masters of the sixteenth, seventeenth, and eighteenth centuries, wherein any of the PIÆ CANTIONES Melodies are to be found, whether in vocal or instrumental arrangement. Reference is also given to some more recent Collections of Carols and Hymns. ¶ For the rest, it is much to Petri's credit that he had the will and the good taste to print, without any desire to modernize, these Melodies (many of which were of considerable antiquity even in 1582); much to his honour, that he rescued from oblivion, and handed down to posterity so valuable a Treasury of Medieval Sacred and Secular Song.

¶ A word of gratitude is due to Mr. Athelstan Riley, the Rev. W. H. Frere, Mr. H. B. Collins, and the late Mr. J. F. H. Woodward, for help in the preparation of this Preface; to the Rev. R. P. Ellis, for reading some of the proofs; to Miss G. B. Jacobi, of Göteborg, for translating several pages of T. Norlind's 'Swensk Historia'; to Mr. C. T. Jacobi, of the Chiswick Press, for sparing no pains over the production of this book; to Mr. E. Fowles, for photographing the old picture on p. 247; and, lastly, to Mr. G. F. Barwick, Superintendent of the British Museum Reading Room, as well as to other officials of that Library, for their usual courtesy in giving the Editor every facility to obtain the material necessary for the furtherance of this work.

CANTIONES

DE NATIVITATE

Domini & Saluatoris nostri
Iesu Christi

I

N-ge-lus e-mit-ti-tur, *A-VE*

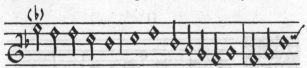

dul-ce pro-mi-tur, se-men De-i se-ri-tur, I-gi-tur

por - ta cœ-li pan-di-tur.

Vim Natura patitur, Filius concipitur,
Virgo non corrumpitur, Igitur &c.

Grex in nocte pascitur, Cœli lumen funditur,
Laus in altis canitur, Igitur &c.

Gaudium prædicitur, Pax quoq, promittitur,
Bonis tamen traditur, Igitur &c.

Nouum ſydus oritur, mortis umbra tollitur,
Mundi ſalus gignitur, Igitur &c.

Diligendus proditur, nil culpandus moritur,
Non vincendus capitur, Igitur &c.

Cruci vita figitur, infernus deſtruitur,
Captiuitas tollitur, Igitur &c.

Adam nexu ſoluitur, mors orco deprimitur,
Caput hoſtis teritur, Igitur &c.

Argumentis igitur in his Chriſtus ſiſtitur,
Morti ſic excluditur. Igitur &c.

II

Er-bū ca-ro fa-ctū eſt de vir-gi-

ne, Ver-bū ca-ro fa-ctū eſt de vir-gi-ne Ma-ri-a.

IN hoc an-ni cir-cu-lo   vi-ta da-tur

se-cu-lo: na-to no-bis par-uu-lo de

vir - gi - ne: na-to no-bis par-uu-lo de

vir - gi - ne Ma - ri - a.

O beata fœmina cuius ventris gloria
Mundi lauat crimina: de virgine Maria.

Stella solem protulit, sol salutem contulit,
Carnem veram abstulit de virgine Maria.

Fons de suo riuulo nascitur pro populo,
Quem tulit de vinculo: de virgine Maria.

Laus, honor, virtus, Domino Deo Patri & Filio,
Sancto simul Paracleto: de virgine Maria.

Resonet

III

E - fo - net in lau - di - bus cum
Chri-ftus na - tus ho - di - e ex
Pu - e - ri con - ci - ni - te, na-
Si - on lau - da Do - mi-num Sal-

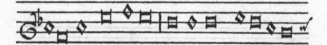

iu - cun-dis plau-fi-bus Si - on cum fi - de-li-bus,
Ma - ri - a vir-gi-ne fine vi - ri - li fe-mi-ne
to re - gi pfal-li-te, vo - ce pi - a di - ci - te
ua - to-rem ho-mi-nũ, pur-ga - to-rem cri-mi-nũ

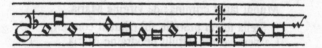

Ap-pa-ru-it quẽ ge-nu-it Ma-ri-a. Sunt im-ple-

ta quæ præ-di-xit Ga-bri-el. E-ya, E-ya, vir-go

De-um ge-nu-it, quem di-ui-na vo-lu-it cle-men-
4 tia.

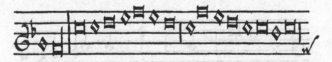

ti-a. Ho-di-e ap-pa-ru-it, ap-pa-ru-it in If-ra-el,

Ex Ma-ri-a vir-gi-ne eft na-tus Rex.

IV

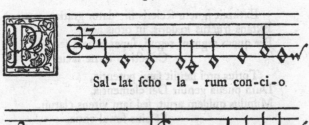

Sal-lat fcho-la-rum con-ci-o

in hoc con-ui-ui-o, Sed Ma-ri-æ Fi-li-

o non fit o-bli-ui-o

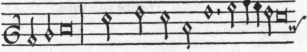

Nam is dat fo-la-ti-a,
5   fua

su - a bo - na gra - ti-

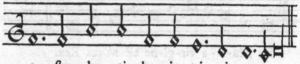

a, stu - den - ti - bus in tri - ui - o.

Extinxit ignem sceleris hic dator gratiæ,
Extans fructus fœderis, in orbis acie,
Per quem regnant reguli, super orbem seculi,
   Cuncti in terræ facie.

Totius orci sæuiit sæui potentia,
Dum puella genuit Dei clementia,
Mundus quidem aruit, sed iam virens claruit,
   Et eius simul entia.

Respexit nos diluculo qui ardet fulmine,
Caritatis oculo à cœli culmine,
Venit huc vt solueret, quos æstus inuolueret,
   Christus suo fulcimine.

Conemur ergo lilij hunc florem legere,
Vt nos partus filij possit protegere,
Hunc omnis felicitas oret et clericitas,
   Vt det nos secum regere.

Certatim laudes concinent cœli palatio,
Christo Iesu iubilent, quos regit ratio,
Hunc omnis deificè collaudet mirificè,
   Triplatæ vitæ statio.

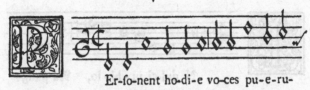

V

Er-ſo-nent ho-di-e vo-ces pu-e-ru-

læ lau-dan-tes iu-cun-dè qui no-bis eſt na-tus,

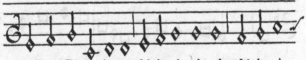

ſum-mo De-o da-tus, & de vir- vir- vir-, & de vir-

vir-, & de vir-gi-ne - o ven-tre pro-cre - a - tus.

In mundo naſcitur, pannis inuoluitur,
Præſepi ponitur ſtabulo brutorum,
Rector ſupernorū, perdidit ſpolia princeps infernorum.

Magi tres venerunt, paruulum inquirunt,
Stellulam ſequendo, ipſum adorando,
Aurum, thus & myrrham ei offerendo.

Omnes clericuli, pariter pueri
Cantent vt angeli, adueniſti mundo,
Laudes tibi fundo. Ideo gloria in excelſis Deo.

In

VI

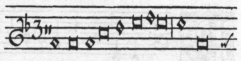

N dul-ci iu - bi - lo, Nu siung-

ge wij ï - o ï - o/ Then all tingh för oß för-

mo lig-ger in præ-se-pi - o, Och som So-len

sfij-ner/ ma-tris in gre-mi - o: Al-pha es &

ω, Al - pha es & ω.

O Iesu parvule för tigh är migh so we/
Tröst migh i mitt sinne O puer optime,
Lätt migh tin godheet sinne O princeps gloriæ,
Trahe me post te, trahe me post te.

8

O

O Patris charitas, O Nati lenitas,
Wij wore plat förderffuadh per noſtra crimina,
Nu haffuer hā oß förwarffuadh cœlorū gaudia,
Eya wore wij thär/ Eya wore wij thär.

Vbi ſunt gaudia Ther ſuinger man/ Eya,
Hwar Englanar ſiunga noua cantica,
Och ſielanar ſpringa in regis curia,
Eya wore wij thär/ Eya wore wij thär.

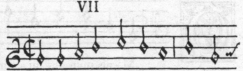

C - ce no-uum gau-di-um,   ec - ce
Vir-go pa- rit   fi - li-um quæ non

no-uum mi-rū,   Quæ non no-uit vi-rum, ſed vt
no- uit vi-rū,   Ec - ce quod na-tu - ra mu-tat

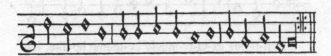

py-rus py-rū, gle-ba ſert pa-py-rū flo-rens li-li-um.
ſu- a iu-ra, virgo pa-rit pu-ra De- i fi-li-um.

Mundum Deus flebilem cernens in ruina,
Roſam delectabilem produxit de ſpina,

9   Produxit

Produxit de spina, natum de regina,
Qui & medicina, salus gentium. Ecce quod, &c.

Nequiuit diuinitas plus humiliari,
Nec nostra carnalitas magis exaltari,
Magis exaltari, Deo coæquari,
Cœlo collocari, per coniugium. Ecce quod, &c.

VIII

M - nis mun-dus iu - cun-de-tur
Ca - sta ma - ter quæ con-ce-pit

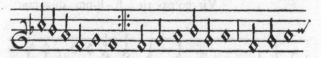

na-to sal-ua-to-re,   syn-ce-ris vo-ci-bus, syn-ce-ris
Ga-bri-e-lis o -re,

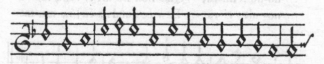

men-ti-bus ex-ul-te-mus & læ-te-mur ho-di-e, ho-

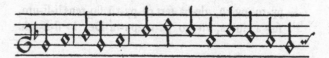

di - e, ho-di - e, Chri-stus na-tus ex Ma-ri - a
10   virgine,

vir-gi-ne, vir-gi-ne, vir-gi-ne, Chri-ſtus na-tus ex

Ma-ri-a vir-gi-ne, gau-de-te, gau-de-te, gau-de-

a-mus & læ-te-mur i-ta-que, i-ta-que, i-ta-que,

gau-de-a-mus & læ-te-mur i-ta-que.

IX

I-es eſt læ-ti-ci-æ   in or-
Nam pro-ceſ-ſit ho-di-e de ven-tre

tu re-ga-li,
vir-gi-na-li,   Pu-er ad-mi-ra-bi-lis, to-tus
delectabilis

de - le - cta - bi - lis in hu - ma - ni - ta - te,

qui in - æ - sti - ma - bi - lis est & in - ef-

fa - bi - lis in di - ui - ni - ta - te.

Orto Dei filio virgine de pura,
Ut rosa de lilio, stupescit natura,
Quem parit iuuencula, natum ante secula,
     Creatorem rerum,
Quòd vber munditiæ dat lac pudicitiæ
     Antiquo dierum.

Mater hæc est filia, pater hic est natus,
Quis audiuit talia, Deus homo natus,
Seruus est & dominus, qui ubiq̣ cominus
     nescit comprehendi,
Præsens est & eminus, stupor eius geminus,
     nequit apprehendi.

In obscuro nascitur, illustrator solis,
Stabulo reponitur, princeps terræ molis.
Fasciatur dextera quæ affixit sydera,
     Et cœlos ascendit,
Concrepat vagitibus, qui tonat in nubibus,
     Ac fulgur accendit.

　　　　　　　　　　Angelus

Angelus paſtoribus, iuxta ſuum gregem
Noɛte vigilantibus, natum cœli regem
Nunciat cum gaudio, iacentem in præſepio,
          Infantem pannoſum,
Angelorum Dominum, & præ natis hominum
          Forma ſpecioſum.

Ut vitrum non læditur, ſole penetrante,
Sic illæſa creditur, poſt partum & ante:
Felix hæc puerpera cuius caſta viſcera
          Deum genuerunt,
Et beata vbera in ætate tenera
          Chriſtum laɛtauerunt.

Mundus dum deſcribitur, virgo prægnans ibat,
In Bethlehem dum naſcitur puer qui nos cibat,
In cœlorum curia canebatur gloria
          Nouæ dignitatis.
Deus in ſublimibus det pacem hominibus
          Bonæ voluntatis.

Chriſte qui nos proprijs manibus feciſti,
Et pro nobis omnibus naſci voluiſti,
Te deuotè petimus, laxa quod peccauimus,
          Ne nos interire
Poſt mortem nos miſeros, ne ſimul ad inferos
          Patiaris ire.

X

On - gau - de - at tur-

ba fi - de - li - um, Vir-go ma-ter pe - pe - rit

fi - li - um in Beth-le-hem.

Ad pastores descendit angelus,
Dicens eis: natus est Dominus in Bethlehem.

Loquebantur pastores inuicem,
Transeamus ad nouum hominem in Bethlehem.

Ad præsepe stant bos & asinus,
Cognouerunt quis esset Dominus in Bethlehem.

In octaua dum circumciditur,
Nomen ei Iesus imponitur in Bethlehem.

Trini trino trina dant munera,
Regi regum sugenti vbera in Bethlehem.

Collyridas simul cum nectare
Benedicat Christus Rex gloriæ in Bethlehem.

Puer

XI

P V -er no-bis naf-ci-tur Rec-tor an-

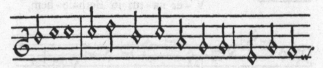

ge-lo-rū, In hoc mun-do pan-di-tur Do-mi-nus

Do-mi-no-rum, Do-mi-nus Do-mi-no-rum.

In præsepe positum Sub fœno asinorum
Cognouerunt Dominum Christum Regem cœlorum.

Hunc Herodes timuit Magno cum tremore,
In infantes irruit Hos cædens in furore.

Qui natus ex Maria Die hodierna
Duc nos tua gratia Ad gaudia superna.

Te saluator α & ω Cantemus in choro,
Cantemus in organo, Benedicamus Domino.

Puer

XII

TENOR

V - er na - tus in Beth - le - hem,

in Beth-le-hem, Un-de gau-det Ie-ru-ſa-lem, Al-

le - lui - a.

BASSVS

PV-er na-tus in Beth-le-hem; in Beth-le-hem, Un-

de gau-det Ie-ru-ſa-lem, Al-le - lui - a.

16   Aſſumſit

Assumsit carnem hominis
Verbum Patris altissimi, Alleluia.

Per Gabrielis nuncium
Virgo concepit filium, Alleluia.

De matre natus virgine
Sine virili semine, Alleluia.

Sine serpentis vulnere
De nostro venit sanguine, Alleluia.

In carne nobis similis,
Peccato sed dissimilis, Alleluia.

Tanquam sponsus de thalamo
Processit matris vtero, Alleluia.

Hic iacet in præsepio
Qui regnat sine termino, Alleluia.

Cognouit bos & asinus
Quòd puer erat Dominus, Alleluia.

Et angelus pastoribus
Reuelat quis sit Dominus, Alleluia.

Magi de longè veniunt,
Aurum, thus, myrrham offerunt, Alleluia.

Intrantes domum inuicem
Natum salutant hominem, Alleluia.

In hoc natali gaudio
Benedicamus Domino, Alleluia.

Laudetur sancta Trinitas,
Deo dicamus gratias, Alleluia.

XIII

D can-tus læ - ti - ci - æ
Na - tus eſt E -ma-nu - el,
Er - go nos cum gau-di - o,

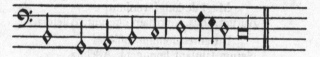

nos in -ui - tat ho - di - e ſpes &
quod præ di - xit Ga - bri - el, vn - de
no - ſtra ſi -mul con - ci - o be - ne-

a - mor pa - tri - æ cœ - le - ſtis.
San - ctus Da - ni - el eſt te - ſtis.
di - cat Do- mi - no iu - bi - lo.

ALTERA VOX

Ad can - tus læ - ti - ci - æ nos
Na - tus eſt E -ma-nu - el, quod
Er - go nos cum gau- di - o, no-
18 inuitat

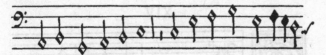

in - ui - tat ho - di - e   ſpes & a - mor pa - tri -
præ di - xit Ga - bri - el,   un - de San - ctus Da - ni -
ſtra ſi - mul con - ci - o   be - ne - di - cat Do - mi -

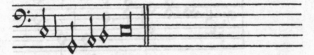

æ cœ - le - ſtis.
el eſt te - ſtis.
no iu - bi - lo.

XIV

Au-de-te, gau-de-te, Chri-stus

est na-tus ex Ma-ri-a vir-gi-ne, gau-de-te.

Tempus adeſt gratiæ, hoc quod optabamus,
Carmina leticiæ devotè reddamus.

Deus homo factus eſt, Natura mirante,
Mundus renovatus eſt à Chriſto regnante.

Ezechielis porta clauſa pertranſitur,
Unde lux eſt orta, ſalus inuenitur.

Ergo noſtra concio pſallat iam in luſtro,
Benedicat Domino, ſalus Regi noſtro.

De

DE RESVRRECTIONE DOMINI NOSTRI IESV CHRISTI

XV

Hri-ſtus pro no-bis paſ-ſus eſt,

& im-mo-la-tus ag-nus eſt, Ef-fu-ſo ſu-o ſan-

gui-ne in ip-ſa cru-cis ar-bo-re, & mor-tu-us

im-pe-ri-um de-ui-cit Di-a-bo-li-cum.

21

Nã

Nā resurgēs ex mortuis, victor redit ex inferis,
Deleuit et chyrographum, nobis quod est contrariū,
Exspoliato Sathana, reclusa cœli ianua.

Habemus ergo liberum iam nos ad Patrē aditū,
Per Christum Dei filium, pro nobis morti traditū,
Alleluia, Alleluia, Benedicamus Domino.

XVI

E - sus hu - ma - ni ge - ne-

ris ex mem - bris na - tus te - ne - ris

vir - gi - ne - is fa - ctus est sal - ua - ti - o,

psal - lat fi - de - lis con - ci - o.

O uis gaudet deperdita, & sanitati reddita,
                                    Vitæ data.
Spreta vi Pythonica, exulta plebs Catholica.

Hamum appendit cœlicum, qui fructum tulit deicum,
Magnificum,
Vincens inferni principem, pendens ad crucis stipitem.

Aspexit nos Sophia exclusos Hierarchia,
Mundi via,
Emisit nobis Filium, laudemus cœli lilium.

Nomen Iesu gloriosum, & verbū Dei generosū
In seculum,
Cuius amara passio est mitis consolatio.

Nostris da Patrem luminum culpis fore propitium
Atque pium,
Ne terreat supplicium, dele peccantis vitium.

E misti tuo sanguine à Stygis nos voragine
Et scelere,
Matris piæ hortamine flentem naturam respice.

Sancto sit laus Paracleto cum Patre simul Filio,
Præ gaudio,
Septem dona Spiritus nobis redde diuinitus.

ACROSTICON, *JOHANNES.*

XVII

E-dit hy-ems e-mi-nus,   sur-re-xit

Chri-stus Do-mi-nus, tu-lit-que gau-di-a: val-lis no-
23   stra

stra flo - ru-it, re-ui-uif-cunt a-ri-da, poft-

quam ver in-te-pu-it, re-ca-lef-cunt fri - gi-da.

Paftor, qui pro ouibus ducendis ab erroribus
Ponebat animam,
Libens ferre voluit crucis pœnam maximam,
Soluit quæ non rapuit, per mortem turpiffimam.

Vidit & condoluit quod ouis vna defuit
Errans per deuium,
In deferto deferit magnam gregem ouium,
Abit, quærit, reperit errantem per deuium.

Magna miferatio, quam reduxit de deuio
Imponit humeris.
Non eft dolor fimilis dolori quem pateris,
Iefu, qui fic humilis factus es præ cæteris.

Mortis nexu diruto, Dracone furgens obruto
Deprædans inferos,
Pharaonis impio captiuos & miferos
Ducens ab imperio, choros ufque fuperos.

XVIII

V-

cun-da - re, ij   iu-

gi - ter plebs de-uo-ta de _ bi - tis

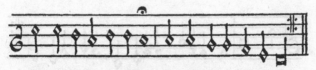

Me-los ca-nens dul-ci - ter ij   ij
Qui te tu - lit a - cri-ter ij   ij

Chri-ſti Ie-ſu me-ri-tis, Chri-ſti Ie-ſu me-ri-tis.
vin -cu-lis ab in -ti-mis, vin-cu -lis ab in -ti - mis.

De

DE TRINITATE

XIX

Ri - for-
Eſt ho-

mis re - lu - cen - ti - a
nor, vir - tus, glo - ri - a

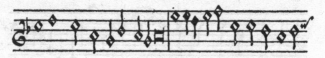

a - bun - dat in ſo - li - o, lu - cis de - fi - ci - en -
v - ni - for - mi ra - di - o, qui ſu - pra re - rum en -

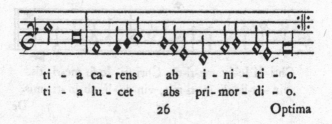

ti - a ca - rens ab i - ni - ti - o.
ti - a lu - cet abs pri - mor - di - o.

Op-ti-ma funt en - ti - a   Op-ti-mam du - cen-

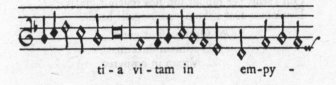

ti - a vi - tam in   em-py -

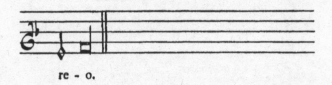

re - o.

Hæc lux mirando lumine, mira triplex affuit,
Seraphico in culmine, formulasque coluit,
Cuncta quæ funt sub tegmine polorum compofuit,
Potentias in homine de non ente ſtatuit. Opt. &c.

O quàm Pater ingenitus excellens potentia,
Patre procedit Filius diues ſapientia,
Ab vtroque manat Spiritus prædulcis clementia,
Hæ tres Perſonæ penitus, ſimplices eſſentia. Opt. &c.

Magnus Deus in opere, maior in Natura,
Potens mira perficere patet in creatura,
Qui polum ſciuit pingere plaſmabili pictura,
Cuncta diſponit pondere, numero et menſura. Opt. &c.

Autor deſcendit cœlitus in caritate pura,
Occultans ſe diuinitus ſub lilij clauſura,
Quidnam admirabilius quam virgo paritura?
Quod Eſaias penitus proſpexit in figura. Opt. &c.

Sol

Sol vertitur zodiaco, gradiens in Geminis,
Dum sol supremus thalamo iuuenescit virginis,
Erupit fons cum balsamo coelicæ dulcedinis,
Rosa creuit de calamo in salutem hominis. Opt. &c.

Fecit grande conuiuium amator castitatis,
Suscipiens homagium nostræ fragilitatis,
Qui carnis per supplicium nos redemit gratis,
Laudemus Dei Filium cum angelis beatis.

      ℟. Optima sunt entia
         Optimam ducentia
         Vitam in empyreo.

ACROSTICON, *THOMAS FECIT.*

De

DE EVCHARISTIA

XX

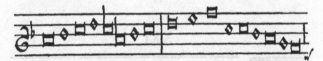

I-ui-num my-fte-ri-um

mo-dò de-cla-ra - tur, & mens in-fi-de-li-um

tu-mens e-xe-cra - tur, fir-ma fpe cre-den-ti-um-

- - - - - fi-des ro-bo-ra - - - - - tur.

Panis primo cernitur, qui, dum confecratur,
Chriftus tunc porrigitur, & fub pane datur,
Quomodo efficitur Chriftus operatur.

Et vinum fimiliter cum fit benedictum
Et tunc eft veraciter fanguis Chrifti dictum:
Credimus communiter verum eft, non fictum.

Fides

Fides est summoperè credere in Deum,
Panem sanctum edere & tractare eum,
Iubet Christus sumere, Hoc est corpus meum.

Nobis celebrantibus istud Sacramentum
Et cunctis credentibus fiat nutrimentum :
Iudæis negantibus fit in detrimentum.

Pater, Nate, Spiritus almum consolamen
Det nobis propitius nostrum restauramen,
Ut cum cœli ciuibus personemus, Amen.

XXI

E-sus Chri-stus no-stra sa-lus,

Quod re-cla-mat om-nis ma - lus, no-bis su-i

me-mo-ri-am de-dit in pa-nis ho-sti-am.

O quàm sanctus panis iste
Quem tu præbes, Iesu Christe,
Caro cibus, Sacramentum,
Quo non est maius inuentum.

Hoc

Hoc est donum sanctitatis
Charitasque Deitatis,
Virtus & Eucharistia,
Communionis gratia.

Aue deitatis forma,
Dei vnionis norma,
In te quisque delectatur
Qui in fide speculatur.

Non solus panis, sed Deus
Homo, liberator meus,
Qui in cruce pependisti
Et in carne defecisti.

Non augetur consecratus,
Nec consumtus fit mutatus,
Nec diuisus in fractura,
Plenus Deus in statura.

Esca digna Angelorum,
Charitasque lux sanctorum,
Lex moderna comprobauit
Quod antiqua figurauit.

Salutare medicamen,
Peccatorum releuamen,
Pasce nos, à malis leua,
Duc nos vbi lux longæua.

O quam magna tu fecisti
Dum te, Christe, impressisti
Panis et vini specie
Obfantium in facie.

Caro cibus, sanguis potus,
Manet tamen Christus totus,
Huic sit laus & gloria
In seculorum secula.

ACROSTICON, *JOHANNES OC=Hus*.

CANTIO PRECUM

XXII

O Rex cœ-lo-rum Do-mi-ne,
Te de-pre-cor, ex-au-di me,

tu mun-di fa-ctor fa-bri-cæ, Nec te la-tent
tu-o re-demp-tũ ſan-gui-ne. Ab al-uo ma-

ſæ-uiſ-ſi-ma quæ com-mi-ſi fla-gi-ti-a.
tris ha-cte-nus ſuc-cur-re Rex pro-pi-ti-us.

Tu es enim piiſſimus, qui de ſupernis ſedibus
Veniſti me redimere: noli peccantem perdere.
Quid proderit, ſi pereo, mihi tua redemptio?
Certè foret vtilius, ne unquam eſſem genitus.

In domo quondam Simonis, tu inceſtae mulieris
Diluiſti facinora, mira nimis clementia:
Tu pius es hæretici miſertus & Theophili,
Quia conuerſus doluit, ſummam mercedem habuit.

Memento, Rex magnifice, qui es dignatus dicere:
Nolo peccantem perdere, fed conuertentem viuere:
Peccator fum, non abnego, idcirco ad te clamito.
Nā potens es dimittere quicquid peccaui, Domine.

O magnæ Rex potentiæ, O pietatis vnice,
Audi preces quas profero tibi pro me miferrimo:
Quis nifi tu me audiat? quis præter te fubueniat?
Si non audis, ad alium non eft recurfus Dominum.

Sit tibi laus & gloria per cuncta, Iefu, fecula,
Qui mifereris omnium ad te piè clamantium:
Eadem laus mitiffimo fit Patri cum Paraclito,
Uni trinoque Domino qui regnat fine termino.

DE BEATA VIRGINE MARIA

XXIII

Ve, re - gi - na om - ni-
Tu vir - tu - tis prin - ci - pi-

um, Ma - ri - a, fa-lus ho-mi-num cre-den-ti-ũ,
um, tu pau-pe-rum re-fu-gi - um, fo - la - ti-ũ,

quæ pau - pe - res fal - ua - re vo - lu - i - fti.
tu ve-rum lu-men mun-do con - tu - li - fti.

Te col-lau-dat ex-er-ci-tus cœ-le-ftis An-ge-lo-rũ

magnificat,

mag-ni-fi-cat, glo-ri-fi-cat & præ-di-cat, a-do-rat

om-nis or-do be-a-to-rum.

Tu solis habitaculum,
Iusticiæ spectaculum, signaculum,
Tu sola Patri semper placuisti,
Tu vitæ propugnaculum,
Tu summi Dei aureum palatium,
Tu caput Holofernis confregisti,
Tu balsami suauitas, tu odor pigmentorum,
Tu charitas, tu castitas, tu bonitas,
Tu fragrans cella plena vnguentorum.

Ad te clamantes respice,
Maria, piè protege & eripe
A laqueo æterno damnatorum,
Mentes ægrorum refoue,
Lapsorum gressus erige & dirige
Ad te tuorum corda famulorum.
Tu lilium convallium,
Tu mala granatorum,
Tu campi flos, virtutum dos, & cœli ros,
Tu perduc nos ad regna supernorum.

XXIV

Al - ue, flos et de - cor Ec-cle
Te fa-ten-tur sa - cræ pro-phe

fi - æ, lu-men hu-ius vi-æ, Ad te cla-mans fi-ti-o;
ti - æ, Vox-que I - fa-i-æ, Pur-am om-ni vi-ti-o.

Virgo fi-ne vi-ro pe-pe-ri - - - - - - - fti,

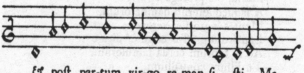

& poft par-tum vir-go re-man-fi - fti, Ma-

ter Ie-fu Chri-fti, qui ca-ret i-ni-ti-o.

36 Hæc

Hæc adeſt ubi periclitatur, verè nuncupatur
            Portus nauigantium;
In ardore rubi præſignatur, & piè vocatur
            Mater deſperantium.
Möyſis hæc ſcirpea fiſcella
Præbens lapſis gratiarum mella, Lucens maris ſtella,
            Via deuiantium.

Subleuatrix pia miſerorum, ad regnum cœlorum
            Duc nos poſt exilium.
Releuatrix pia peccatorum, rectrix ſupernorum
            Da ſanum conſilium.
O dulcis, O clemens atque pia,
Sis nobis directrix atque via, in extremis, dia,
            Fer nobis auxilium.

XXV

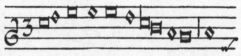

Ir - go ma-ter pi-iſ - ſi-ma cun-
Tu mi-hi ſis cer-tiſ- ſi-ma ſal-

cto - rum plaſ-ma-to-ris,   Sis, om-ni-bus in ho-
ua - trix pec- ca-to-ris.

ris, te cor-de fla-gi-tan-ti-um, & o-re col-laud-
                                     dantium

dan - ti-um sti-pen - di-um la-bo-ris.

Præcellit rosa lilium candore puritatis,
Virgo adorat filium, quem parit, castitatis;
Hæc sydus claritatis, hæc balsamo süauior,
Sole, luna splendidior feruore charitatis.

Virtutum flos & gratiæ aures ad nos inclina,
Placata Patris facie, charismata propina,
Nos à mundi sentina celerius eripias,
Et tecum nos custodias in vnitate trina.

XXVI

Sal - lat   fi-de - lis con-
Et præ - sen-te -mus can-

ci-o cum gau-di-o iu-bi - lan-do Ma-ri-æ,
ti-ca or - ga -ni-ca so-len- nis me - lo-di-æ.

38   Quam

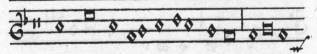

Quam ſi - ne la - be cri - mi-nis et ſal-uo
Per quam gu-ſtus e - xi - ti - j & per-pe-

flo - re vir - gi-nis ma-trem Pa-ter e-le-git:
tis e - xi - li - j ius pri - ſti-num in-fre-git.

Tu es pin-cer - na ve - ni-æ di-ues in
Tu ſtel - la pu - di - ci - ti-æ, tu vi-tæ

cha - ri-ta-te, Et fons mi-ſe - ri-cor - di-æ
me-di-ci-na, Pec-ca - ti te - lo ſau - ci-æ

ma-nans ſu-a - ui-ta-te. O no-bi-lis
mun - di - ci-æ cor-ti-na. Et mor-ta-li-

puerpera

pu-er - pe-ra, mun-di tu la-uas fce-le-ra, hoc
um ge - ne - ri clau-fi-fti por-tas in-fe-ri, ve-

or - bi per - fe-ci-fti,　　Flos vir - gi-num,
ctef-que con - fre-gi-fti.　　Tu fer - uu- lis

dux ag - mi-num cœ-le-fti-um præ cæ-te-ris
pe - ri - cu- lis re-fu-gi- um cœ- le-fti-bus

ho-mi-ni-bus be-a-ta. O re- gi - na fi -
ag-mi-ni-bus præ-la-ta. Stel-la ma - ris ap-

ne fpi-na tu ro-fa ver-na - lis, Dans o-do-
pel-la-ris lap-fis in fen-ti - nam, Pec-ca-to-

　　　　　　　　rem

rem dul - ci - o - rem Pa - ra - di - si ma - lis,
rum nau - fra-go- rum di - ri - ge ca - ri -nam

Tu gem-ma prin-ci-pa-lis,   Sig-num du-mi,
Ad pa - tri - am di-ui-nam.

vir - ga fu - mi, vi - gor æ - sti - ua - lis.

In qua do - mo nul - lus ho-mo pa-ti-tur ru-i-nam.

Ma-ri- a, fa-lus ho-mi - num, me-di-ci -
Nam ex te ma-nat gra-ti - a, Pax, mi-fe -

41   na

na cri - mi - num, Te de - cet poſt Do-
ri - cor- di - a, fi - des, tem - pe - ran-

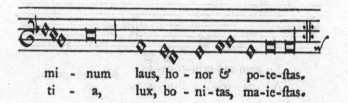

mi - num laus, ho - nor & po - te - ſtas.
ti - a, lux, bo - ni - tas, ma - ie - ſtas.

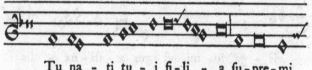

Tu na - ti tu - i fi - li - a ſu - pre - mi

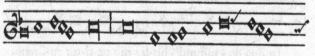

ge - ni - to - ris, Con - ti - nen - tis om - ni-

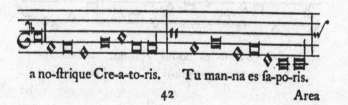

a no - ſtrique Cre - a - to - ris. Tu man - na es ſa - po - ris.

Area

A-re-a a-ri-da, quam fu-per-nus hu-mor ir-ri-
Tu fi-ne fe-mi-ne Na - ti De- i ma- ter ex-fti-

ga-uit, Vi-ne-a re-gi-a, ro-fa fpi-næ ne-fci-a quam
ti-fti, Cœ-li-cos a-di-tus, ve-ti-tos in-tro- i -tus or-

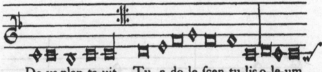

De-us plan-ta-uit. Tu a-do-le-fcen-tu-lis o-le-um
bi re-clu - fi - fti. Tu nau-tæ flu-&ti-ua-go fi-dus fa-

ef-fu-fum, Sa-lus in pe-ri- cu - lis, fpes in of-
lu-ta- re, An-cho-ra tu nau-fra-go, fub-mer-fis

fen-di-cu-lis, o - fti-um præ-clu-fum. Tu prin-
in pe-la-go nobis au-xi - li - a - re. Fle - &te

43

cipium

ci-pi-um no-ſtræ ſal-ua- ti - o -nis, Re-duc de-
ri-gi-dum mun-da-nis in-hæ-ren-tem, Fo-ue fri-

(♭)

ui-um ad thro-num Sa-lo - mo - nis. Im-pe-
gi-dum à cri - mi - ne tor-pen - tem.

tra di-ui-ni-tus, ap-plau-de lau-dan-ti-bus & in

te ſpe-ran-ti-bus Vi-tam cum be - a - tis. Ut ſub-

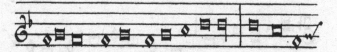

la-tis pe-ni-tus pœ-nis in-fer-na-li-bus, iun-

gamur

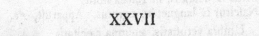

ga-mur ag-mi-ni-bus De-o fo-ci-a-tis.   O

ma - ter pi - e - ta - tis.

XXVII

Ve, ma - ris ftel - la, Di-

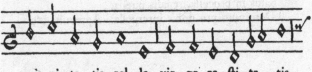

ui - ni - ta - tis cel - la, vir - go ca - fti - ta - tis,

ra-dix fa-ncti-ta-tis, ge-ni-trix æ-ter-næ cla-ri-

tatis.

ta-tis. ℟. Ap-pa-ru-it, ap-pa-ru-it quem pi-a

Vir-go ge-nu-it Ma-ri-a.

Hominum saluator, et angelorum sator,
Mitis & deuotus, in Iudæa notus
Nascitur & languet vt ægrotus. Apparuit, &c.

Umbra vetustatis, ænigma cæcitatis
Transiit in lucem, virga profert nucem,
Israel dat ex Ægypto ducem. Apparuit, &c.

Rigor perit legis, dum pro peccato gregis
Pastor immolatur, hostia mactatur,
Populus in tenebris salvatur. Apparuit, &c.

Ave, singularis, Maria, stella maris,
Salus in procella, regalis puella,
Dominum pro nobis interpella. Apparuit, &c.

Ave

XXVIII

Ve ma-ris ſtel – la
De – i – ta-tis cel – la

lu-cens mi-ſe-ris,
por- ta prin-ci-pis,

Pa- ra-di – ſi pa-tens fons tu cy-preſ-ſus, Si-on
Pa-tris ſub um-bra-mi –ne Ver-bum ca- ro fit per

mons,   pec- ca - to-rum pons.
te,   Sa-cro fla-mi – ne.

47   Regis

Regis diadema, stola præsidis,
Samsonis problema, funda Dauidis,
Turris per quam transit gens, Deū verū tenens ens,
                  ne desperet flens.
Tu es Salomonis res, in te tota nostra spes
                     agitur per tres.

   Mater pietatis, spes fidelium,
Ebur castitatis, candens lilium,
Urna cœli, manat ros, in te creuit Iesse flos,
                   Qui saluavit nos.
Rubus quem non urit pyr et in cuius ponit ir
                 Se cœlestis vir.

De

DE FRAGILITATE

& miserijs humanae
conditionis

XXIX

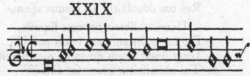

A-ni - ta-tum va-ni-tas, om-ni-a

funt va - na, Nil fub fo-le fta-bi-le in vi-ta hu-

ma - na, ve-lut fu-mus tran-fi-it glo-ri-a mun-

da-na, i-fta cur am-ple-cte-ris, O tu mens in-fa - na?

Cæcus es? an oculus tibi caligauit?
Et apertis oculis cæcitas proftrauit,
Vel tuam dementiam furor indurauit?
Ifta non confideras, neque cor expauit.

Dic, miser homuncule, quidnam cogitasti?
Cuius erunt omnia hæc quæ congregasti?
Ad caput reponitur tibi quod amasti?
Nequidquam: sed possides id quod ignorasti.

Animam Diaboli rapiunt ad pœnas,
Amici pecunias diuidunt amœnas,
Vermes carnem deuorant simul atque venas,
Res tua deuoluitur ad manus alienas.

Uxori & liberis res tuas liquisti,
Pro his miser animam tuam posuisti,
Uxor ducit alium quem tu non nouisti,
Tui obliuiscitur quam sic dilexisti.

Sic perit memoria tuorum filiorum
Ipsis succedentibus in prosperis bonorum,
Gaudent cum gaudentibus, vt mos est eorum,
It tui memoria cum sonitu verborum.

XXX

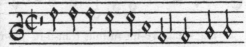

N-sig-nis est fi-gu-ra quam ad in-
Am-bi-gu-a sta-tu-ra cu - ius ru-

ue-nit a-ri-es, Cun-&o-rū flos cam-po-rū, mū-dū vo-
go-sa fa-ci-es, a - spe-ri-tas mem-bro-rū, vi - tæ præ-

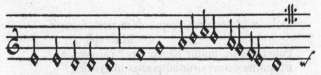

can-do ve-tu-lam, gref-fu mi-   ra-bi - lem.
fen-tisfor-mu-lammon-ftrat in-   fta-bi - lem.

Con-ftat cun-&is cer-tif-fi-mè iam to-ti-es ex-per-

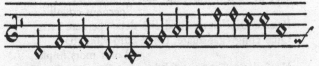

tum quod de-flu-it ci-tif-fi-mè fi-nem ha-bens in-

cer-tum; hanc er-go cre-das fa-bu-lam,   rem tàm

pro   -   ba - bi - lem.

O quàm multa promittit, longã vitã, diuitias,
Fauores & honores, tandem in fine decipit
                              Te fallibiliter.
Nam nudum te dimittit ad maximas miferias,

51   Dolores

Dolores & horrores, corpus dum terra suscipit
                              Miserabiliter.
Possessio disrumpitur hæredes per carnales,
Et anima demergitur ad pœnas infernales,
Scito quis ista recipit iam satis grauiter.

  Quàm miser es, auare, qui non vis Deo credere,
Nec in eum sperare, qui diligis terrestria,
                              Spernens cœlestia.
Prædico tibi clarè, quod citò debes perdere
Quæ congregas auarè, teque cum violentia
                              Tollit mors impia.
Versutias, astutias persoluis cum usura,
Post carnisque delitias quas possides cum cura,
Traheris ad supplicia semper manentia.

  Si tamen vis saluari, innixus Christi sanguine,
Dum tempus indulgetur, pietatis operibus
                              Insta fideliter.
Misericors placari Pater potest facillimè:
Si tamen exoretur: nam lachrymis & precibus
                              flectitur dulciter.
Nam si conuersus fueris corde simul & ore,
Tuaque libens dederis diuino cum amore,
Verè cum sanctis omnibus viues feliciter.

Mirum,

I-rum, ſi læ-te - ris, dum ex ap-
Mors fal - lax So-phi-ſta, bre-ues di-

pa-ren-ti-bus ma-gis quàm ex ve - ris, Mors con-
es ho-mi-nis: quàm ve - ra ſunt i - ſta! in - tus

clu - dit & il - lu - dit, ho-mo quid tunc e - ris?
a - ret & di-ſpa-ret fra - gi - lis a - ri - ſta.

Cum ſi-ne vi-ti-js ho-mo vix in mun-do, heu

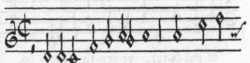

ſit ſup-pli-ci-js in la-cu pro-fun - do a-gi-ta-tur

& pul-ſa-tur, vt ven-tis a-run - do.

Mors mundi figura,
Quæ corrupta ſubitò perit, vt pictura,
Non in luctu, ſed in fluctu hominem demtura.
O mundi Sophia,
Nos errantes corrige veritatis via,
Ut eamus, ne cadamus in mortis ruina.
Tu ſpes humilium, rutilans aurora,
Pro nobis Dominum iugiter implora,
Adiuvare tu dignare nos mortis in hora.

Hominem tàm durum
Iacentem in crimine, ſe iudicaturum,
Dum poſt mortem ſciat fortem iudicem venturum,
Quid artes? quid iura
Tibi proſunt homini? ſolùm ad futura
Vel eſt *Ite* vel *Venite* iudicis cenſura.
Ergo dum veneris, Iudex, iudicare,
Tu noſtri generis ſtatim memorare,
Quos emiſti, redemiſti, noli condemnare.

XXXII

men-tes per - 'fi-das & lin-guas

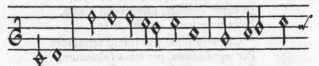

du - pli-ces, & te-ftes fub - do-los, & fal - fos iu -

di-ces: au-ra-tè fa - bri-cant frau-dum ar-

ti - fi-ces in dor-fo pau - pe-rum fer-rum

et fi - li-ces.

Impunè frangitur fides in publico,
Vix poteft credere priuignus vitrico,
Vix pater filio, vix æger medico,
Ipfe, qui conqueror, in fide claudico.

Ubique

Ubique timeo dentem vipereum;
Venenum seminant vendentes oleum;
Qui tecum loquitur trahit ad laqueum,
Ut tibi temperet doloris balneum.

Nullus nocentior hoste domestico,
In magno decipit sicut in modico,
De non ambiguis apertè iudico,
De fratris laqueo vix pedem explico.

Si bonum fecerim, occultè lacerat,
Si malum aliquid, fingens exaggerat,
Si verum approbo, in multis peierat,
Ut prosit hostibus, amicos vulnerat.

Minatur filio mortis in radio,
In visu Regulus, in cauda Scorpio,
In dente coluber, princeps in gladio,
Ficta simplicitas in falso labio.

Clamore super hos infero terminum
Per ægritudines, per ictus fulminum,
Romana curia fouet periuria,
Pro nummi gratia saluat mendacia.

XXXIII

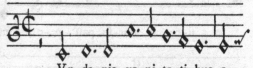

Vn-da-nis va-ni-ta-ti-bus a-
E - la - tus fa-cul-ta-ti-bus re-

stri-ctus po - ten-ta-ti-bus,   Nam sa-pi-ens
si - stit cum dog-ma-ti-bus.   Sunt i-sta tran-

        sic

sic in-ſtru-it, ſer - ui -re ma-gis con-gru-it ve-ris
ſi - to- ri - a, ſper-nen-da ve-lut ſco- ri-a prop-ter

fe - li - ci-ta-ti-bus, ab - ie - ctis fal - ſi
cæ- li pa - la-ti -um, ve -rum ga - zo - phy-

ta - ti - bus.
la - ci - um.

Vorax infernus ſurripit ſuis nos ſuaſionibus,
Conſentientem corripit æternis torſionibus,
Mundus extollit leuiter illos quos fallit breuiter,
Mortem ponens in foribus multos pulſat timoribus.
Carnalis vrget macula perurens quaſi facula,
Multi pro tanto vitio torrentur in ſupplicio.

Traduntur in hiſtorijs viri digni memorijs,
Virtutibus eximijs fulſerunt & ſcientijs,
Cunctis locis & viculis ponentes ſe periculis,
Spreuerunt hic terreſtria, amplexi ſunt cœleſtia,
Præclari Solis radio certabant in hoc ſtadio,
Patris Abrahæ gremio funguntur vitæ præmio.

Quorum ſcholares ſtudio benignè vos erudio,
Hæc vobis ſit concluſio, vana deſit confuſio,

In

In mentē nam maleuolam, deformem siue friuolā
Non intrat Sapientia virtutum seu decentia.
Clamans inquit Sagacia, per mundi cuncta spacia,
Vitam bonam comperiet homo qui me reperiet.

XXXIV

O-ne-sta-tis de -cus iā mu-ta-
Heu in-dig-ni quæ-runt sub - li-ma-
Fi-des a - mi-co-rum iam va-cil-
Au-di, fi - li, mo -rum dis - ci - pli-

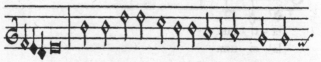

- tur, oc- cul-ta-tur ve-ri-ta-tis splen-dor per
- ri, vt lu-cra-ri sub-di-to-rum va - le - ant.
- lat, & ti - til-lat cor e - o - rum a - du - lans
- nam, & do-ctri-nam Sa-lo-mo-nis at-ten-dens.

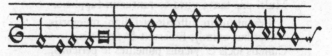

men-da - ci-a, con-cul- ca -tur ca-sti-ta-tis ro-sa
pe -cu - ni-as: stra- ta nam-que vi-ti-o-rum he-u
fal - la - ci-a, cū pro-pi - nat fel pro mel-le per ver-
cor in - cli-na, vt se-cu-rus Sal-ua-to-ris se-qua-

sub lux-u - ri-ta, om-nis æ-tas, fex-us, or-do
per-dunt a - ni-mas, & e - ge - nos pri-uant bo-nis,
ba præ-dul-ci-a, o - re plau-dant & ap-plau-dant
ris ve - fti - gi - a: ti-me De-um, pla - ca e-um,

ftu-det a - ua - ri - ti - æ, tran-fit æ-tas mo-rum,
nec dant e-lee-mo-fy-nas : fed po-ten-tes di - tant
fi - bi per con-ui-ti - a, cor-de frau-dant me-di-
pur-ga no-xam la-chry-ma, præ-fto fis & o - ra

cor - de com - ple - &un - tur vi - ti - a.
do - nis prop - ter a - mi - ci - ti - as.
tan-do: hæc nunc a - mi - ci - ti - a.
e - um vt du - cat ad gau-di-a.

59   Scribere

XXXV

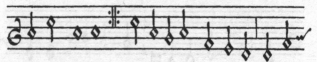

Cri-be-re pro-po-ſu-i   de con-tem-
Iam eſt ho-ra ſur-ge-re de ſom-no

tu mun-da-no: Zi-za-ni-am ſper-ne-re ſum-to
mor - tis va-no,

vir-tu-tum gra-no: Sur-ge, ſur-ge, vi-gi - la, ſem-

per e - ſto pa - ra - tus.

Ubi ſunt qui ante nos in hoc mundo fuêre?
Venias ad tumulum ſi vis eos videre:
Cineres & vermes ſunt poſtquam computruêre.
Surge, ſurge, vigila, &c.

In hoc mundo naſcitur vir omnis cum mœrore,
Atꝗ vita ducitur humana cum labore,
Poſt extremum clauditur cum funeris dolore. Surge &c.

Vita

Vita brevis, breviter in breui finietur,
Venit mors velociter, & neminem veretur,
Omnia mors furripit, & nulli miferetur. Surge &c.

O fi fcires gloriam in Regno beatorum,
Nunquam dares animam ad vana mundanorum,
Sed feruires iugiter Rectori angelorum. Surge &c.

O quâ felices hi funt qui cum Chrifto regnabunt,
Facie ad faciem dum ipfum infpectabunt,
Sanctus, Sanctus Sabaoth Domino proclamabunt. Surge &c.

O quàm dolor flebilis à Chrifto feparari,
Et nunquam in numeris iuftorum nominari,
Sed femper in tenebris inferni cruciari. Surge &c.

O fi pœnam minimam fentires damnatorum,
Benè vim hîc fufferres cunctorum tormentorum,
Ut fic poffes fugere dolores captiuorum. Surge &c.

Ibi nullam requiem acquirunt exiftentes,
Nec laffantur Dæmones animas punientes,
Quorum voces clamitant, Væ, Væ æternaliter.
Surge, furge, vigila, femper efto paratus.

XXXVI

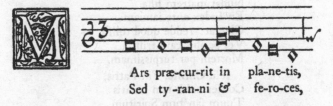

Ars præ-cur-rit in pla-ne-tis,
Sed ty -ran-ni & fe-ro-ces,

ho-mo pa-cis & qui-e-tis nil va-let in fe - cu-lo:
qui ad ma-la funt ve-lo-ces hireg-nant in po-pu-lo:

Effrenes

Ef-fre-nes & in-do - mi-ti, qui de-ua-ſtant &

in-cen-dunt, quæ ſunt ſu-a non at-ten-dunt, ta-

les pla - cent co - mi-ti.

Ducunt vaccas, equos, boues,
Capras, hircos, porcos, oues,
Et ſi qua ſimilia.
Ducunt lanum atq̄ linum,
De rapinis implent ſinum,
Nudat matrem filia.
En Iudex ante ianuam
Clamat: redde quod tuliſti,
Vel peribis caſu triſti,
Mortem per turpiſſimam.

Ieſu Chriſte, Fili Patris,
Confer nobis iam renatis
Tuum ſanctum Spiritum.
Quid prodeſſet nobis naſci,
Si tu velles Rex iraſci
Ad noſtrum interitum?
Memento quod ſumus tui,
Tu es factor, nos factura,
Tibi ſit pro nobis cura,
Te precamur cernui.

Inualuit

XXXVII

N - ua - lu - it ma - li - ti - a
De - fpi - ci - tur iu - fti - ci - a

iam ho - ra ve - fpe - ra - rum:
v - bi - que nunc ter - ra - rum.

Cre-fcunt cre-bro vi-ti-a re-rum mun-da-na-rum,

Eft con-cors ad fup-pli-ci-a i-ma-go di-

- - - - - ui - na-rum.

Ocello luftrat fingula Naturæ vim pertranfiens,
Duelloq; fubtilia fophifmatum difcutiens,
Cum mundi huius machina et gyrum cœli ambiens,
Quæritq; fic magnalia feipfum homo nefciens.

Amat nunc mundus dulciter honores populares,
Erigitq; fuauiter ad gradus clericales,
Fallit tandem breuiter quos iam fecit tales,
Nec velut pridē nequiter nunc fallit, immortales.

Exurgens iam reuertere, O dulcis mî amica,
Emendemus nos hodie ne moriamur ita,
Ad pedes Iefu fuftine, imago infignita,
Nil tibi fit amabile nifi ipfius vita.

XXXVIII

Vm fit om - nis ca - ro fœ-
Cer - ne quid es, quid et e-

num, & poft fœ - num fi - at cœ-num, ho -
ris; mo - dò flos es, fed uer-te- ris in

mo quid ex-tol-le-ris?
fa - uil - lam ci-ne-ris.   Ter - ram te-ris, ter-ram

geris

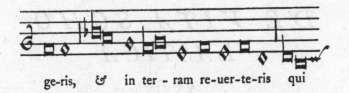

ge-ris, & in ter - ram re-uer-te-ris qui

de ter - ra fu - e - ris.

Homo dictus es ab humo;
Citò transis, quia fumo similis efficeris.
Nunquam in eodem statu
Permanes dum sub rotatu huius vitæ
    volueris.   Terram teris &c.

Homo nascens cum mœrore,
Vitam ducens cum dolore, & cum metu moreris,
Te memento moriturum,
Et post mortem hoc messurum,
Quod hic seminaueris.   Terram teris, terram
    geris, & in terram reuerteris qui de terra fueris.

DE VITA SCHO-
LASTICA

XXXIX

A - sti - ta - tis spe - cu - lum,

Scho-la - res, a-ma — te, re-lin-quen-tes se-

cu-lum scho-las fre-quen - ta - te, pu-e-ro-rum

ru-di-men-ta pre-cor vt co-la - tis, & vir-tu-tum

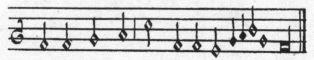

in - cre - men - ta ſum - mè di - li - ga - tis.

Boëtij

Boëtij studia iubent amouere
Veneris incendia, nec in his gaudere:
Assumatur pro exemplo Lucretiæ natus,
Corrigatur sic extemplò iuuenilis status.

Commessationibus sed heu iam assuescunt,
Suis lectionibus omninò marcescunt;
Sicut causæ & causati se contingunt sedes,
Sic sunt Bacchus fœderati atq Ganimedes.

Intricatis vestium gaudent ornamentis,
Et suorum crinium toruis polimentis,
Gulam suam decorare fuco concupiscunt,
Magistratum honorare pauci iam addiscunt.

Tabulatis calceis incedunt elati,
Et in semicirculis gyrant ut inflati:
Nolunt Scholis interesse, truphis inhiantes,
Sed festinant his abesse, vanis ambulantes.

Vitia dementiæ, scholares, fugate,
Nectare Scientiæ vos inebriate,
Totu nisu custodite morum honestates,
Et æternæ vobis vitæ dentur dignitates.

XL

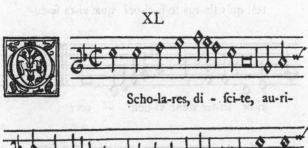

Scho-la-res, di - sci-te, au-ri-

bus per-ci - pi-te, o-cu-lis vi-de - te, quàm be-

atam

ā-tam du - ci-tis vi-tam, quàm di-li - gi-tis

ftu-di-um qui-e - tis. Ma-nè Scho-las pe-ti-

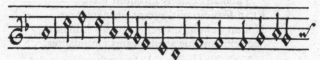

te, ve-ſpe-ri re-ce - di-te do-mum re-pe-ten-

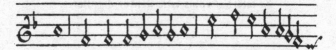

tes: quis ſta-tus fe-li-ci-or? quæ vi-ta ſe-cu-

ri-or in-ter nunc vi-uen - tes?

Reges, duces, comites, principes & milites
Nunquam ſunt ſecuri.
Viuunt enim miſerè, arma debent gerere,
Semper pugnaturi.

Appellantur

Appellantur Domini: omini non homini
    Talis laus debetur.
Bona tranfitoria funt eorum gloria,
    Sicuti videtur.

Mercatores auidi, nocte, die timidi
    Flumina marina,
Propter lucrum tranfeunt, & quandoq̃ pereunt
    Morte repentina,
Quorum mercimonia forte pendent dubia,
    Paritur & vita.
Vifu miferabili pereunt de facili
    Diu acquifita.

Ruftici funt afini quibus terræ Domini
    Dominantur mirè.
Quicquid habent, rapiunt; fi non habent, adigunt
    Pauperes abire.
De Thefauro paupere magnis folent addere
    Magnam portionem.
Sed eò flebilius quòd his Deus citius
    Mittat vltionem.

Regula Scholarium eft excellens omnium,
    Vitæ fanctitate,
Licet nulla fimilis, tamen eft difficilis
    In afperitate:
Soli Deo feruiunt, fitiunt, efuriunt,
    Quorum paupertatem
Enarrare nequeo, confequunter ideo
    Chrifti pietatem.

Ex iftis colligite vitam, quam diligite,
    Semper clericalem.
Singula pertranfeo ita quòd nunc nefcio
    Similem vel talem.
Vos eftis in medio, libero arbitrio
    Ritè confidentes,
Poftquam fenueritis, Sacerdotes eritis
    Deo feruientes.

           Qui

Qui in terris proprium linquunt patrimonium,
 Habent ſpiritale:
Quapropter ſollicitè date preces debitè
 Propter donum tale:
Ipſe vos ad gaudia transferat cœleſtia,
 Precibus placatus,
Vbi ſine termino hymnum canit Domino
 Populus beatus.

XLI

Cho-la-res, con-ue-ni-te, li -
Tra-cta-bo vo-bis ri-tè, quæ,

ben-ter hæc au-di-te, pro-cul a vi-ti-o. Nam
qua-lis ve-ſtræ vi-tæ con-ſtet con-di-ti-o. Vix

pri - mi-tus bar-ba-ti, in fa-ci-e ru-ga-ti,
vo - lunt ab-la-cta-ti iam eſ-ſe ſub-iu-ga-ti

ſtabant

sta - bant ri - go - ri - bus.
fu - is do - cto - ri - bus.

En quondam timuiſtis Magiſtros, dum ſediſtis
Vos in pulueribus:
Tunc certè profeciſtis cum ſubditi fuiſtis
Scholæ verberibus.
Omne caput langueſcit dùm paſtor oues neſcit
Ac errans erit grex:
Latinum iam receſſit, barbaricum acceſſit,
Scholarum perit lex.

Scholaribus reuera pecunia in pera,
Quinterna manibus,
Et capitis in ſphæra mitra fulget ſyncera
Modis in omnibus.
Vix ſciunt *G*, *Vt*, *A*, *Re*, nec *Muſa* declinare,
Nec curant ſtudium:
Sed diſcunt chorizare, incipiunt amare
Mundi tripudium.

XLII

I - ſci - pli - næ fi - li - us
Fra - ter, cur ſis de - ui - us,
E - ſto No - e ſi - mi - lis,
For - te ſum o - di - bi - lis,

ait.

a - it im - per - ter. - ri - to,
cur fu-das in ve - ti - to?
con - fe-cra - tus Do - mi - no:
qui - a ve - rum con - ci - no.

Pa - ti - en - ter

pa - te-re   ver-ba cum fla-

gi - ti - js, no - li du - ra fper — ne - re,

ne vol - ua - ris vi - ti - js, ne vol - ua - ris

vi - ti - js.

72   Timor

Timor est initium omnis sapientiæ,
Timor fugat vitium vilis ignorantiæ,
Timor dat fastigium regiæ potentiæ,
Timor est humilium clypeus in acie. Patienter &c.

Quid nocet id perdere quod tàm citò redeat?
Quidnam cutem vendere, cum citò refloreat?
Pro cute recipere quod plus auro valeat:
Ergo, frater, patere quòd te timor arceat. Patienter&c.

Dulcia non meminit qui non gustat tristia,
Mel [vt Plato cecinit] sapit post absynthia.
Nam Mattheus concinit inter Euangelia,
Vbi timor desinit, incipit miseria. Patienter &c.

Sicut humor modicus est medela floribus,
Sic et timor medicus optimus in rudibus:
Taurum domat Rusticus ictu, fuste, restibus,
Puerum Scholasticus verbis & verberibus. Patienter&c.

Nunquam Pharaonicus proficit in artibus,
Quia Diabolicus talis est in omnibus:
Iam ad finem contraho, velut ambo sapimus,
Si vis esse Pharao, finis erit pessimus. Patienter &c.

XLIII

IN sta-di-o la-bo-ris
Sed bra-ui-um ho-no-ris

cur-runt om-nes so-ci-j:
non se-quun-tur sin-gu-li.

Si non vis o-ne-rari,

ra - ri, ca - ue - as ho - no - ra - ri: ho - nor vult o-

ne - re gra - ua - ri.

Sicut dulcedo mellis non euacuabitur,
Acerbitasque fellis nunquam relaxabitur,
Sic & in prælatura nullus eſt ſine cura:
      Rerum hoc exigit Natura.

Sed, ſi in libertate viuere volueris,
Viuas in caritate, ſic tu non dolueris.
Nil habes, nil dolebis, perditum neq flebis,
      Sed in hoc quod habes gaudebis.

XLIV

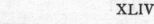

Cho-la mo - rum flo - ru-it
Sta-tim flos   e-mar-cu-it,

dùm ti-mo-rem ha - bu-it: ʃed ti-mo - re
nec flo-re - re po - tu-it, mox ti-mo - re
         mortuo

mor - tu-o,
de - flu-o.   Ti-mor, ho-no-ris vin-cu-lum,

in-ftru-it di-fci-pu-lum. Er-go, fi vis in - ftru-i,

fer ti-mo - ris iu - gu-lum, & do - cen -tis

ba - cu - lum,   quem re - pel - lunt fa - tu - i.

Timor laudabilium honor eft Scholarium,
Pauperes magnificat.
Timor dat imperium, rudium ingenium
Docet & autenticat. Timor &c.

Timor habet ordinem ad fupremum cardinem,
Vbi nemo litigat.
Timor manfuetudinem excitat, & turbinem
Punientis mitigat. Timor &c.

Timor

Timor & attentio fint Scholis in precio.
Puer qui affumferit,
Puer in hoc biuio, fi floret ingenio,
Triumphare poterit. Timor &c.

Timor eft in inferis, quo concordant fuperis;
Nam fine Concordia
Error eft in cæteris: hæc funt verba veteris,
Qui timebat omnia. Timor &c.

Timor ei poculum, vitæ habitaculum.
In æterna gloria
Dat, fi hunc tenuerit ipfumq fapuerit,
Æua per folatia. Timor &c.

XLV

Vm in a-li-e-na   pro-

uin - ci-a, con-tur-bat me mi-fe-ri-a, iam

de-fi-cit fub-ftan-ti-a, e-ua-nu-it læ-ti-ci-a, e-

uanuit

ua - nu - it læ - ti - ci - a.

O Sal-ua - tor   mor - ta - li - um,

con-fo-la-tor fi-de - li-um, Per te De-us nos fal-

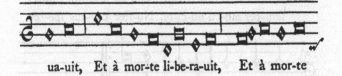

ua-uit, Et à mor-te li-be-ra-uit,   Et à mor-te

li - be - ra - uit.

De prouincia fum expulsus, in angaria fum deftructus,
Iam factus fum vt laicus, conftringit me viliffimus.

Miles effem, equitaffem; latro effem, fpoliaffem;
Nõ fum latro neq̃ miles, fed Phœbi pauper Satelles.

Monachus

Monachus effe non valeo, Eremita non audeo,
Mendicare erubefco, & fodere iam nequeo.

O Saluator mortalium, confolator fidelium,
Per te Deus nos faluauit, & à morte liberauit.

XLVI

Scho - la - res, vo - ce pa - res,
Et cho - re - am iu - bi - le - am

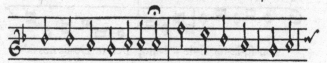

iam me-cū con-ci-ni-te. Iam ad fe-ftum mo-dò
fem-per me-cū du-cị-te, No-fter cœ-tus fpe-ret

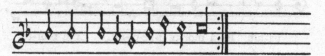

mœ-ftū fer-ui-tu-tis ftu-di - j.
læ-tus no-bi-lis con-ui-ui - j.

Conuiuari, non triftari, iubet lex in feculo:
Confolari, iucundari mandat Bacchus populo.
Ergo gaude, plaude, laude, concio fcholarium:
O fi tale, tale, tale femper effet gaudium!

Felix ludus, in quo nudus fcholaris verberibus
Non fuccumbit, nec decumbit magiftri liuoribus.
Ergo gaude, plaude, laude, concio fcholarium:
O fi tale, tale, tale femper effet gaudium!

De

Hac - - - - - - - - -

- - - - O quàm mun-dum, quã iu-cun-dum
- - - - hac vir - tu - te funt fo - lu - tæ

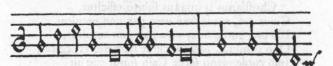

vi - ue-re con-cor — di-ter, Nam Pfal-mi-fta
res u-ni-tæ for — ti-ter, iuf - fu o - ris

ver - ba i - fta lo - qui - tur ve - ra — ci-ter.
Cre - a -to- ris vi - uunt re - gu-la — ri-ter.

Herus

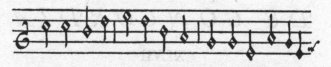

He-rus ve-rus fert fyn-ce-rus: fan-&i funt pa-ci-

fi - ci, gra - ti, na - ti, non vo-ca - ti, fi-unt hi

de - i - fi - ci.

Chriftianus is infanus fubitò efficitur,
Cuius ore, corde fore vera pax non cernitur.
Illo ore, corde fore, vera pax non cernitur,
Quo coniurat, patrem curat fternere, vt legitur,
Ipfo corde pleno forde Cain fimul corruit
Vehementer, fraudulenter, dum in fratrem irruit.

Hanc in facto nuper acto, Scarioth non habuit,
Dum lethale, heu tàm male, laqueo fe induit:
Magnũ donum, fummũ bonũ confert pacis dignitas:
Tollit bella, cordis fella, mentis fit fynceritas.
Eft amoris vinclum foris, optima felicitas,
Premit iras intus diras: oris eft fuauitas.

Lætemur

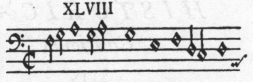

Æ-te-mur, om-nes fo-ci - j,

pfal - len-tes cum tri - pu - di-o: In no-ftro fit

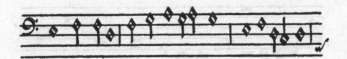

con-for-ti-o fyn-ce-rus a - mor, ve-ra fi - des,

pro-cul i - ra & in-dig - na - ti - o.

Benignam vitam ducite in huius fecli tramite,
Omnes dolos abijcite, virtutes bonorum
Ac honeftatem morum, ex actis ipforum, colligite.

Te, Christe benigne, laudeq digne, precamur
Euelle fcelera, da nobis iã præterea tales, qui deuotè
Deo famulentur, ad aftra leuentur & æthera.

HISTORICAE
Cantiones
XLIX
PRIMA VOX

A-chæ-us ar-bo-ris a-ſcen - dit

ſti - pi-tem, vt Ie-ſum cer-ne-ret cœ-lo -

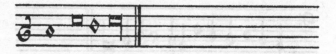

rum ho-ſpi-tem.

ALTERA VOX

ZA-chæ-us ar-bo-ris a-ſcen - dit ſti-pi-
tem,

tem,   vt Ie-fum cer-ne-ret cœ-lo - rum

ho - fpi-tem.

Zachæus Iefum fufcipit hofpitio,
Et caritatis pertractans officio.

Illic perpendens cordis habitaculum,
Si quenquam defraudaui, reddam quadruplum.

Dimidium bonorum do pauperibus,
Placatur Deus talibus muneribus.

Et nos, de tali lætantes conuiuio,
Benedicamus Dominorum Domino.

Tibi nunc quoque, Chrifte, qui nos fatias,
Semper dicamus gratiarum gratias.

Homo

L

O-mo qui-dam Rex no - bi-lis,

di-ues in ca - ri-ta-te, cœ-nã mag-nã di-ui -

ti - js & mag - na lar - gi-ta - te fe - cit,

vo-ca-tis plu-ri-mis, cor-dis hi-la-ri-ta - - - te.

Tempus adeſt, conuiuium vt intrent inuitati,
Regale beneficium contemnunt ſed ingrati:
Sic verum perdunt gaudium mundanis implicati.

Unus ad quem Rex miſerat ıuum fidum legatũ,
Vxorem quòd adduxerat, inuenit occupatum,
Venire nec aptus erat ad feſtum præparatum.

Alter quẽ Rex per nunciũ rogans juſſit intrare
Ad locum exultantium, & epulas guſtare,
Spernens Regis imperium ſic cœpit excuſare.

Domum

Domum altā ædificem, in qua gaudens manebo,
Alteram & amplificem, & plures possidebo,
Si venero, multiplicem defectum hinc habebo.

Rex, ad amicum tertium seruum velociorem
Mittens, rogat vt Regium non deserat amorem,
Sed derelinquens ocium eius seruet honorem.

Respondit: quinq debeo iuga boum probare,
Quæ fortia possideo & ea valdè carè,
Cum quibus opes studeo & terras dilatare.

Tota die lucrum quærens boues defatigauit,
Sed serò quòd quiesceret locum lassus optauit,
Et tenebras dùm cerneret, noctem multā expauit.

Neglectum tunc conuiuium incœpit cogitare,
Regis & ad palatium iam tardè properare,
Clausum inuenit ostium, iubetur foris stare.

Tunc Rex auersa facie dixit, huc non intrabis,
Nec epulas læticiæ vel cœnam hanc gustabis;
Sic tuæ negligentiæ dispendia portabis.

Iam priuor beneficijs, & filijs carebo,
Uxore cum delicijs, & mecum permanebo,
Pernoctans in miserijs, & inde magis flebo.

Mundus, caro, dæmonia me malè seduxistis,
Dùm per diuersa vitia me miserum duxistis,
Et Paradisi ostia finaliter clausistis.

Fratres, hortor perpendite tormenta grauiora,
Assiduè dirigite ad bona meliora,
Ad cœnam vos disponite, nam breuis vocat hora.

Cœlestis Pater gratiæ, qui Christum huc misisti,
Tu nos ad cœnam gloriæ voca à mundo tristi,
Nobiscum stes in acie, amore Iesu Christi.

De

DE TEMPORE VER-
nali Cantiones

LI

I N ver-na-li tem-po-re, or-
Dùm re-ce-dunt fri-go-ra, nun-

tu læ-ta-bun-do, Ter-ræ, ma-ris, ne-mo-ris
ci-at hi-run-do, Vi-gor re-dit cor-po-ris,

de-cus a-deſt de-fo-ris, re-no-ua-to mun-do.
ce-dit do-lor pec-to-ris, tem-po-re iu-cun-do.

Terra vernat floribus & nemus virore,
Aues mulcent cantibus & vocis dulcore,
Aqua tempeſtatibus caret, aër imbribus,
Dulci plenus rore.
Sol conſumtis nubibus, radijs patentibus
Lucet cum dulcore.

O

O quàm mira gloria, quantus decor Dei,
Quanta resplendentia suæ faciei,
A quo ducunt omnia, ima, summa, media,
Formam speciei!
Maior est distantia quàm sit differentia
Noctis & diei.

LII

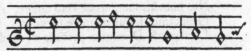

Em-pus a-dest flo-ri-dum, sur-gunt
Ver-na-les in om-ni-bus   i - mi-

nam-q flo-res,
tan-tur mo-res,   Hoc, quod fri-gus læ-se-rat, re-

pa-rant ca-lo-res, cer-ni-mus hoc si-e-ri per

mul-tos la-bo - res.

Sunt

Sunt prata plena floribus iucunda aſpectu,
Ubi iuuat cernere herbas cum delectu,
Gramina & plantæ [quæ] hyeme quieſcunt,
Vernali in tempore virent & accreſcunt.

Hæc vobis pulchrè monſtrant Deum Creatorē,
Quem quoque nos credimus omnium factorem:
O tempus ergo hilare, quo lætari libet,
Renouato nam mundo, nos nouari decet.

Terra ornatur floribus & multo decore,
Nos honeſtis moribus & vero amore,
Gaudeamus igitur tempore iucundo,
Laudemuſq Dominum pectoris ex fundo.

SVPPLEMENTVM

DE NATIVITATE
DOMINI & SALVATORIS
NOSTRI IESV CHRISTI

LIII

E   [de] ra - di - ce
Quæ   [quæ] mi-rum flo-

pro-cef - fe-rat   Ief-fe vir-ga mi - ri - fi-
rem gef- fe-rat,   fœ-cun-da vi De - i - fi-

ca,   Hu-ius vir-gæ   my-fte-
ca: Flos Chri-ftus eft   in fe -

       rium

ri - um   fi fa - ne vis   per - ci - pe-
cu - lo   dans o - do-rem   fu - a - ui-

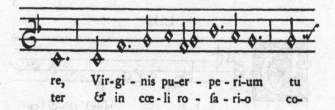

re,   Vir-gi - nis pu-er - pe - ri-um   tu
ter   & in cœ-li ro - fa - ri-o   co-

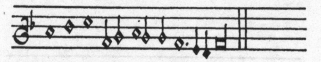

de- bes in-tel - li - ge-re.
ruf-cans æ -ter - na - li -ter.

In fructum flos conuertitur | guftando falutiferum,
Hoc eft corpus [meum] dum loquitur | natus ante luciferum.
Granum, de cuius fructibus | egens turba reficitur,
Chriftus pro nobis omnibus | cadens in terra moritur.
Flos Chriftus eft in feculo | dans odorem fûauiter,
Et in cœli rofario | corufcans æternaliter.

       Lætetur

LIV

Æ
Pax

te - tur Ie-ru - sa-lem, Si-on plau -
in ter-ra co - mi-nus, Lux in noc -

dat fi - li - a. Nam Chri-ftus in
te cla - ru-it, Rex & re-gum

Beth - le-hem na - tus eft fa -
Do - mi-nus mun - do dum ap -

mi - li - à. In Ma-ri-æ fi - li - o no-
pa - ru-it.

ftra

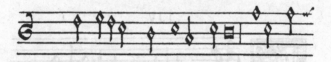

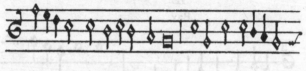

ſtra gau - det con - ci - o, in hoc

ip - ſo par - uu-lo, ſal - ua-to -

re Do - mi-no.

In cœlorum ſedibus regnat & hîc cernitur,
Mitigatur fletibus, heu à multis ſpernitur:
Ibi feliciſſimus in ſupernis colitur,
Hîc vero mitiſſimus in præſepe ponitur. In Mariæ &c.

Exultarunt angeli nato Dei filio,
Exultemus ſinguli in iſto exilio,
Nam humano generi ſalus & redemptio,
Ortus ſalutiferi venit ab initio. In Mariæ &c.

Ipſe fecit hominem & eum pœnituit,
Atqᵃ fudit ſanguinem & peccata abluit.
Pneumati Paracleto detur laus & gloria,
Cum Patre & Filio per æterna ſecula. In Mariæ &c.

De

DE PASSIONE
DOMINI NOSTRI
IESV CHRISTI

LV

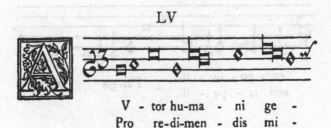

V - tor hu-ma - ni ge -
Pro re-di-men - dis mi -

ne - ris, pi - e - ta - tis mi - ra -
fe - ris, mor - ti da - tis, fu - o

bi - li con-fi - li - o, Na-tum Ma-
non par-cens fi - li - o. Qui paf - fus

ria

ri - a   vir-gi-ne   mor-ti cru-cis
si - ne   cri-mi-ne   ex -ſol-uit quæ

ex - po- ſụ - ıt,   Ful-get   cru-cis
non ra - pụ - it.

my-ſte - ʀ-um,   æ - ter-næ lu-cis ſpe-

cu-lum,   Cui ſub - di-tur im-pe - ri-

um re - Cto-rum hu - ıus ſe - cu-lı.

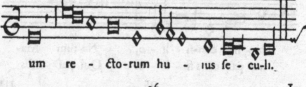

In

In Pa-ra-di-fi gre - mi - o lig-num

vi-tæ, pro-du — &tum, No-ftri la-bo-

ris præ-mi-o, fa-lu - tis pro-fert fru -

&tum. Ag-nus hæ-rens in ve - pri-

bus pro I-fa-ach, oc-ci - di - tur.

H 97 Anguis

An-guis, ſpe-ctan-dus om-ni-bus, cru-

ce pen-dens e-ri - gi-tur. Hæc eſt

a - ra ſa-lu-ta - ris, ri - ga-ta ri-uis

ſan - gui - nis, Qua, Chri - ſte, ſa-

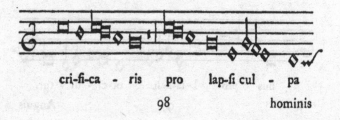

cri-fi-ca - ris pro lap-ſi cul - pa

hominis

ho - mi-nis. Cru-ci cla-uis af-fi -

ge-ris, tu Pa-trem pla-cans ho - sti -

a. Sic con - fi-xus e - ri - ge-ris,

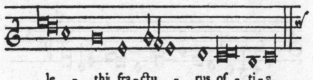

le - thi fra - ctu - rus of - ti - a.

Di-sten - di-tur in sti - pi-te cru-cis,
Of-ten - di-tur in ca - pi-te sa-cro

99   caro

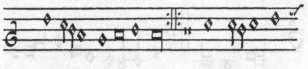

ca-ro   vir-gi-ne - a,   San-guis &
co-ro - na ſpi-ne - a.   Sic mi - ſe-

un - da pro - flu-it de foſ - ſi fon-
ris crux pro - fu-it, quam in - no-cen-

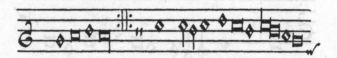

te la-te-ris;   Hoc ex - al-ta - tus
ter pa-te-ris.

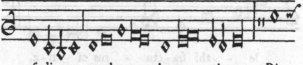

ſo-li - o ut ad te tra - has om - ni - a. Ri-

xæ de-ſtru - &ctto   ſo-li - o fers

ad

ad am-ple - xus bra - chi - a.　　Cor ad

a - man-dum a - pe-ris,　in - cli-nans os

ad of - cu - la;　Suf-fers　pla-gas dum

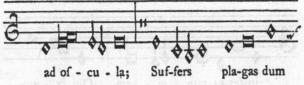

ca - pe-ris,　ſpu - ta, fla-gel - la, vin - cu-la.

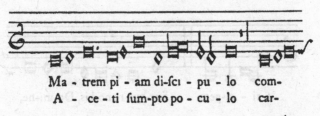

Ma - trem pi - am di-ſci - pu - lo　com-
A - ce - ti ſum-pto po - cu - lo　car-

mendans

men - dans, Pa-tri fpi - ri-tum,
nis ex - fol-uens de - bi-tum.   Sic

mor • te mor - tem de - ſtru-is   vin-cens

in-fer-ni prin - ci - pem,   Qui la - tro-

nem   in-ſti - tu-is   tu - i reg-ni   par-

ti - ci-pem.   Suc-cur-re no-bis, Do-mi-ne,

qui

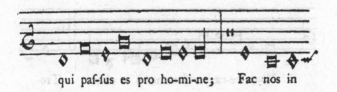

qui paſ-ſus es pro ho-mi-ne; Fac nos in

tu-o Nu-mi-ne fru-i cœ-le - ſti lu-

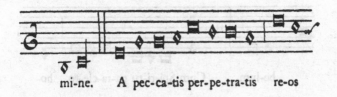

mi-ne. A pec-ca-tis per-pe-tra-tis re-os

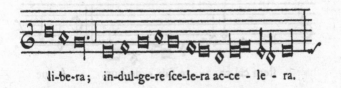

li-be-ra; in-dul-ge-re ſce-le-ra ac-ce - le - ra.

Ti-bi gra-tos & be-a-tos pi-os ef-fi-ce.

Vitæ

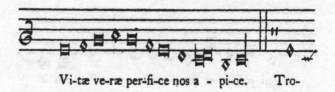

Vi-tæ ve-ræ per-fi-ce nos a - pi-ce.   Tro-

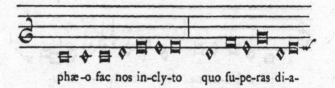

phæ-o fac nos in-cly-to   quo fu-pe-ras di-a-

bo-lum,   Cum Spi-ri-tu pa-ra-cle-to   ho-

ftem cal-ca - re fub - do-lum.   A - ue

crux, tur-mæ dux, for-ma pœ-ni-ten-ti-æ,

tu pec-ca-to-rum ve - ni - a.   In te ſpes &

re-qui-es, nor-ma pa-ti-en-ti-æ, cœ-lo-rum

tan — gens mœ - ni - a.   No-ſtræ

ſa - lu - tis an-cho-ra,   tu por-tus in nau-fra-

gi-o. Qui mun-di pla-cas æ-quo-ra, pa-cis

105   dato

da-to suf-fra - gi-o.　　Tu ve-xil-lum re-
　　　　　　　　　　　　Tu fi-gil-lum le-

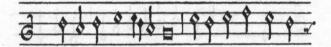

gis es vi - Éto-ri - æ, de-co-ra-tum dig-nis
gis de-cus glo-ri - æ fub-li-ma-tum fig-nis

lo-cis, do-ti-bus.　　Ab ho-ftis ma-lig-ni
& vir - tu-ti-bus.　　Vt Ie - fu be-nig-ni

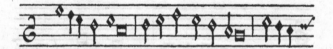

fal - la-ci-a, at-q͗ per-ui-ca-ci-a vir -
nos gra-ti-a du-cat ad fo-la-ti-a fa -

tu - tis de-fen-de nos po - ten-ti-a,　Qui
lu - tis co-len-dæ cum cle-men-ti-a.　V-.

　　　　　　　regnat

reg - nat in cœ-lis cum An-ge-lis ex-al-ta-tus
bi grex fi-de-lis arch - an-ge-lis ſo-ci-a-tus

ſi-ne ter-mi-no.   Cui æ-ter-na cum
ca-nit Do-mi-no.

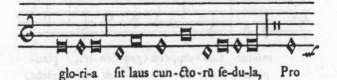

glo-ri-a   ſit laus cun-ꞓto-rū ſe-du-la,   Pro

ſu-per-na vi-ꞓto-ri-a, in ſe-cu-lo - rū ſe -

cu-la.   Can- ta -te can-ti-ca, ſo-ci - j,
               Con-ſor-tes tan-ti ne-go-ti- j,

107   crucis

crú-cis fig-na - ti cha-rá-cte-re; Cul-pæ
læ -te-mur pa - ri-li fœ-de-re. Vi-ta

li-be-re-mur, mun-de-mur, pur-ge-mur à fo-
re-pa-ra-ta, be - a-ta, do-na-ta re-ci

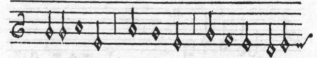

mi-te: Lau - des, con-gau-den-tes, plau-
pi-tur. Dum no-stræ co -hor-tis plebs

den - tes, pfal-len - tes de-pro-mi-te.
mor-tis à por - tis e - ri - pi-tur.

Chri-ftum du-cem, qui per cru-cem nos ad
Cun´-ctis lo-cis, pi - js io-cis, dul-cis

lucem

lu-cem du-xit gra-ti-æ, Ve-ne-re-mur, i-
vo-cis cla-ro ſtu-di-o, Per-ſo-ne-mus, de-

mi-te-mur, gra-tu-le-mur læ - ta fa - ci-e.
can-te-mus, iu-bi-le-mus cum tri-pu- di-o.

Pa-ter, Na-tus, Sa-crū Fla-men, det no-bis ſpē

& ſo-la-men. Nos ve-ni-ens ad ex-a-men

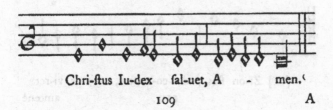

Chri-ſtus Iu-dex ſal-uet, A   -   men.

dex-

Ad - ue-

tris De - i Do - mi - nus, i-
nit no - bis co - mi - nus, ho-

ni - ti-um qui se - det & in æ-
stem sca-bel-lum po - nens pe-dis sæ-

uum, Ex
uum.

[ex] Zi-on flos, dul-co-ris ros, vir-ga vi-ret

amœné

a-mœ - nè.   Ro-fam fpi-na pa-rit ex-

pers pœ - næ, à qua gra-ti-a-rum

flu-unt ve-næ, cu-i cor fi-de-le di-cat be -

nè.

Hic creuit & in tegimen
Nec non cunctorum dominationem,
Cœli terræq̃ regimen,
Abs labe viri incarnationem
Cœpit, vt nos effemus dos
Æternitatis plenè. Rofam fpina &c.

Hic damna ligni reparat
Surgendo, scandit compar Patri digno,
Viam salutis præparat,
Scelus ob nostrum mori volens ligno.
Sis nobis dux, hostis ne trux
Orci nos iungat pœnæ. Rosam spina &c.

Ut agnus insons mutuit
Coram tondente, dixit Esaïas:
Assa caro perduruit
In ligno crucis torrido, Messias
Sic iuuet nos, ne Ditis os
Voret ardore plenè. Rosam spina &c.

LVII

- Mo-ris o - pu-len - -
Ex-pul-sus sum ab om - -

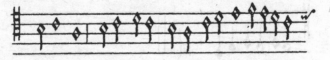

ti-am   Chri - stus mor - te te-sta -
ni-bus   vt ' ex - ul cum ex-u - li-

tur,   ad ve-ram pœ-ni-ten - ti-am   su-
bus; mæ-stum de su - is do -mi-bus   ex -

os sem - per hor-ta - tur: Au - di - to

pel - lunt me cum ca - ni-bus.

quod re - pen - di - tur, cœ - lo - rum

Rex of - fen - di - tur.

Remotis meis veſtibus ſum funibus ligatus,
Iniuſtè victus teſtibus, flagellis flagellatus;
Amaris paſſionibus iuncturas diſſoluebant,
Gingiuæ tūſionibus oris intumeſcebant,
Rumpuntur venæ tactibus, aſſiduis incurſibus.

Alapis cæſa centies eſt veneranda facies,
Coägulatus quinquies ſanguis deformat ſpecies,
Intitulatur paſſio, honoris exhibitio:
Angore cor inficitur, cruci corpus affigitur,
Pedes perfoſſi pondera portarunt ſalutifera.

Latus ferro transfigitur, ſpinis punctus arguitur,
Extenſa membra tenera, pendent nudata viſcera;
Naturæ ſolui debitū, Patri commendans ſpiritum.
Attende qualem exitum ſum paſſus & interitum,
Diſcurre probans omnia quòd nemo curat talia.

O qualis retributio, contrarij commiffio,
Magiftratus defpectio pro charitatis ftudio,
Infelix finis talium, æterna mors ftipendium,
Nautarum exclamatio fum femper & probatio,
Ut Samfon fortis viribus oro pro peccatoribus.

Suäuis Deus, omnium miferere peccantium,
Tales vermes occidere quid tibi pro hoc gloriæ?
Eis magis compatere, tu, Pater omnis gratiæ,
Convertere laudabilis, & efto deprecabilis.
Vbi mifericordiæ? Dauidis in progenie.

Memorare fubftantiæ, Pater, tuæ familiæ,
Affatur Patrem Filius, quod vix fiat celerius,
Miferebor ramufculis Dauid fugatis vitijs,
Æternitatis cellulis locans pro pœnitentijs,
Nobis optati taliter regnabunt æternaliter.

LVIII
DISCANTVS

tas,

114   ætas

æ - tas car-men me - lo - di - æ

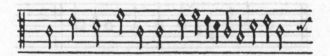

pſal-lat, lau-dem in Meſ - ſi - - -

- æ, can-ti-co læ - ti-ci - æ. Nam-

que, nam - que dig - nus eſt ho-no - re,

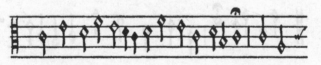

qui pla-ca - uit paſ-ſi-o - ne Pa-trem

omnis

om-nis gra - - - - - - - - - - - -

- - - - - - - ti - æ.

Æ - - - - - - - -

- - - - tas, æ-tas car-men me -

lo - di - æ pſal-lat, lau-dem in Meſ-ſi -

116   æ,

— — — æ, can-ti-co læ-ti - ci-

æ. Nam - que, nam-q̃ dig-nus eſt ho -

- no-re, qui pla-ca - uit paſ-ſi - o - ne

Pa-trē om-nis gra - - - - -

- - - - - - - ci - æ.

Baſſvs

Æ - - - - - - - -

- - - tas, æ-tas car-men me -

lo-di - æ pſal-lat, lau-dem in Meſ-ſi -

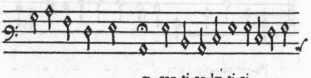

- - - - æ, can-ti-co læ-ti-ci -

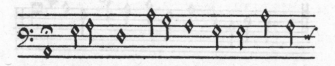

æ. Nam - q̃, nam - q̃ dig-nus est ho-

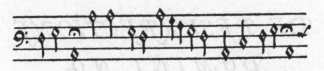

no - re, qui pla-ca - uit   paf-fi - o - ne

Pa-trem om-nis gra - - - - -

ti - æ.

De

DE RESVRRECTIONE
DOMINI NO-
STRI IESV
CHRISTI

LIX

DISCANTVS

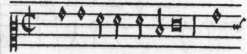

E-dit hy-ems e - mi-nus, fur-

rex-it Chri-ſtus Do - mi - nus tu-lit-q̃ gau-

di - a, val-lis no-ſtra flo-ru - it, re-ui-uiſ-cunt

arida

a - ri-da, poft-quam ver in-te-pu-it re-ca-

lef-cunt fri - gi-da.

TENOR

Ce-dit hy-ems e - mi-nus, fur-rex-it Chri-

ftus Do - mi - nus tu-lit-q̃ gau-di - a, val-

lis no-ftra flo - ru-it, re-ui-uif-cunt

arida.

a - ri - da, poſt-quam ver in-te-pu-it, re-ca-

leſ-cunt fri - . gi - da.

BASSVS

Ce-dit hy-ems e-mi-nus, ſur-rex-it Chri-ſtus

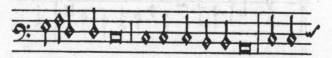

Do - mi-nus tü-lit - q̃ gau-di - a, val-lis

no-ſtra flo - ru - it, re-ui-uiſ-cunt a - ri-da,

poſtquã

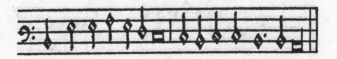

post-quã ver in-te-pu-it,   re-ca-lef-cunt fri - gi-da.

LX

DISCANTVS

V - - - - -

- - - - - - cun-da-re ij

iu - - gi - ter, plebs de-uo-

'ta, de - - bi-tis,   Me-los   ca-nens
                     Qui te   tu- lit
dulciter

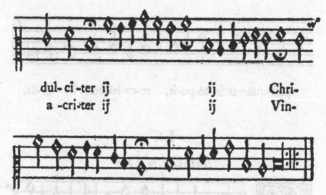

dul- ci -ter ij   ij   Chri-
a -cri-ter ij   ij   Vin-

sti Ie-ſu me - ri - tis, Chri-ſti Ie - ſu me-ri-tis,
cu-lis ab in - ti - mis, Vin-cu-lis ab in-ti-mis.

TENOR

Iv - - - - - - -

cun-da - re ij   iu - - -

gi - ter, plebs de-uo-ta, de - - bi-tis,

       Melos

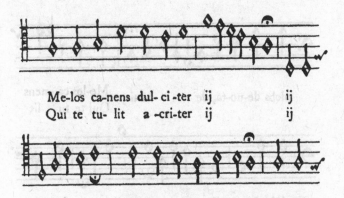

Me-los ca-nens dul-ci-ter ij ij
Qui te tu-lit a-cri-ter ij ij

Chri-fti Ie-fu me-ri-tis, Chri-fti
Vin-cu-lis ab in-ti-mis, Vin-cu-

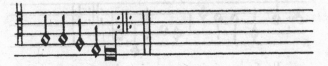

Ie-fu me-ri-tis.
lis ab in-ti-mis.

BASSVS

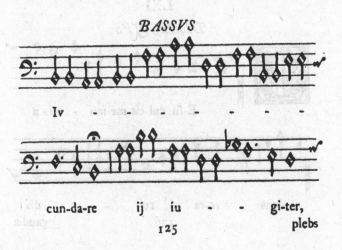

cun-da-re ij iu - - gi-ter,
plebs

plebs de-uo-ta, de - bi-tis, Me-los ca - nens
Qui te tu - lit

dul- ci -ter ij ij Chri-sti
a -cri-ter ij ij Vin-cu-

Ie - fu me-ri-tis, me - ri -tis,
lis ab in-ti-mis, in - ti - mis.

LXI

DISCANTVS

E-fu dul-cis me-mo - ri - a

dans ve-ra cor - dis
gaudia

gau-di - a; Ie-ſu dul-ce-do cor-di-um, fons

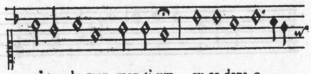

vi-tæ, lu-men men-ti-um, ex-ce-dens o -

- mne gau-di-um.

ALTVS

Ie-ſu dul-cis me - mo-ri - a   dans ve-ra

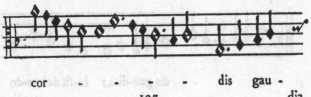

cor -   -   dis   gau -

dia

di - a: Ie-ſu dul-ce-do cor-di-um, fons vi-tæ, lu-

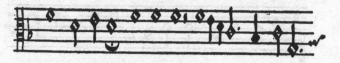

men men-ti-ũ, ex-ce-dens om-ne

gau-di-um.

TENOR

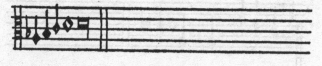

Ie-ſu dul-cis me - mo - ri - a dans ve-ra

cor - - dis gau-di-a: Ie-ſu dul-ce-do

128   cordium

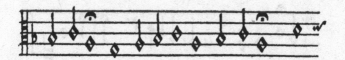

cor-di-um, fons vi-tæ, lu-men men-ti-um,   ex-

ce-dens om -   -   ne gau-di-um.

BASSVS

Ie-ſu dul-cis me -   mo-ri-a dans

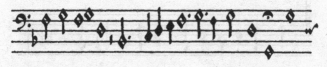

ve-ra cor-dis   ij   gau-di-a: Ie-

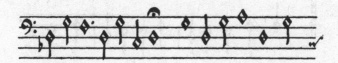

ſu dul-ce-do cor-di-um, fons vi-tæ, lu-men men-

ti-um, ex-ce-dens om ne gau-di-um.

Sed fuper mel & omnia eius dulcis præfentia,
Nil canitur fuäuius, auditur nil iucundius
Quàm Iefus Dei filius.

Iefu mî bone, fentiam amoris tui copiam,
Iefu largitor veniæ, honor cœleftis patriæ,
Tu fons mifericordiæ.

LXII

dul-cis Ie-fus, fpi-nis læ-fus, fla-

gris cæ-fus a - fpe-ris, ve-lis pla-ca - tus fo-re.

Qui, lux de lu-ce, vi-cto du-ce, pen-dens
cruce

cru-ce sce-le-ris, in-du-tus es splen-do-re.

In - fer-ni por-tas ur - gens, in-de tu-os du-
Post tri-du-um re - sur-gens, mun-di vi-ctor fu-

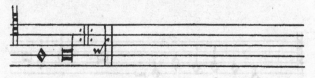

xi - sti.
i - sti.

In

IN FESTO PENTE-
COSTES

LXIII

Van-do Chri-ſtus aſ-cen - de-rat,

ſe-dens ad Pa-tris dex-te-ram, quem an - te-a

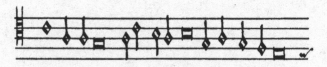

pro-mi-ſe-rat, è cœ - lo mit-tit Spi-ri-tum,

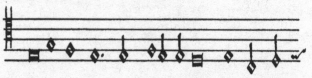

au-di-tur tan-quam ſo - ni-tus, lin-guis lo-

quuntur

quun - tur om - ni-um.

Hic subitò adueniens metum incuſſit omnibus,
Et conſolatur pauidos Apoſtolorum animos,
Qui ſtatim linguis varijs docent Dei magnalia.

Fœcundat hic Eccleſiam diuerſis donis ſterilem,
Conſolatur, illuminat & ſeruat conſcientiam,
Aduerſus mūdum, Sathanam & diræ mortis impetum.

Patrem oramus igitur cœleſtem, Sanctū Spiritum,
Ut nos in fide Filij pura ſemper retineat,
Alleluia, alleluia, benedicamus Domino.

De

DE TRINITATE

LXIV

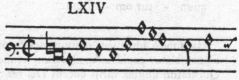

E   —   [be] ne-
E   —   [be] ne-

di-ci-te   Tres   Per - ſo - nas   Tri-ni-
di-ci-te   Do-mi-num   cre-an - tem   om -

ta - tis   v-num eſ-ſe De - i ta - - tis, à quo
ni - a   v- ni-uer-ſo-rum   en - ti - a   ſic tres

ſub-ſi - ſtunt   om-ni-a   re-rum ſi - mul en-
in for - na - cis me-di-o   o - di-zant cum tri-

tia
tia

- ti-a, Hunc De - - um be-ne-di - - ci-te.
pu-di-o, Hunc De - um be-ne-di - - ci-te.

Et Chri-ſtum De - - i fi-li -li-um, ac ſan -
Et nos in hoc con-ui-ui- o *Be - ne -*
Lau - de - tur ſan - &ta Tri-ni-tas *De - o*

&tum quo- q̷ Spi - - ri-tum,
di - ca - mus Do - - mi-no, Can-tan - tes
di - ca - mus *gra - - ti-as,*

Be-ne - di - - ci-te.

Benè

LXV

E - [be] nè quon-dam

do-ci-les Scho-la-res mi-ra - ri cœ-pe-runt

mi-ra-bi-les vi-den-tes cre - a - ri res & has

dif-fi-mi-les a-ctus o-pe-ra - ri. Cœ-

[cœ]-pit A - ri-fto-te-les his

miris

mi - ris phi - lo-so-pha - ri.

I n intelligentiam primi entis verè
Senſus per noticiam veteres venêre,
Quo primam eſſentiam res omnes ſumſêre,
Affirmarunt quoniam nil poſſe creante carere.

R ident licet phyſici de Philoſophia,
Quanto plus Catholici, qui ex Prophetia
Fiunt ſcientifici, non ex phantaſia,
Nam data multiplici fit eis virtute Sophia.

C redimus ſtabiliter fide non creatum
Patrem æternaliter generaſſe Natum,
Et Flamen æqualiter ab vtroq latum;
Unum, tres pariter, ſunt hi ſuper omne creatum.

E xpedit Grammaticis leuiter tranſire
In rebus Deificis quàm quid definire,
Ne queant Hæreticis noſtri conſentire,
Sitq Theologicis iudicare facilè de re.

R egem Deum credimus trinum in Perſonis,
Quem præeſſe nouimus malis atq bonis,
Nequaquam concedimus tres Deos in Thronis:
Sed Deus eſt unus, Angelorũ canitur ſonis.

V t poſſimus fidere Trinitatem eſſe,
Simplicibus ſapere non plus eſt neceſſe,
Quàm valebunt metere fidei de meſſe,
Imo minus capere docti reputant facilè ſe.

S cholares in triuio ſtudentes guberna,
Regnans ab initio, Trinitas æterna;
Fac vita cum gaudio frui ſempiterna,
Puros nos à vitio ducês ad regna ſuperna.

ACROSTICON, BIRCERVS.

137

De

DE BEATA VIRGINE MARIA

LXVI

Lo - rens iu-uen - tus vir -

gi-nis fru-ctum sa-lu-tis ger-mi-nat. Qui

la-ben-tis o - ri - gi-nis ve-tu - sta-

tem ex-ter-mi-nat. Dum ver-bum Pa-tris na-

scitur

sci-tur ex ma - tre si-mul fi-li-a, Fac-tum-q

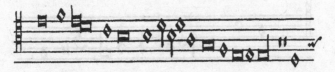

ca-ro paſ - ci-tur in-ter pu-do-ris li-li-a. In

fi - ne vir - go tem - po-ris mem-bris tu-

me - ſcit te-ne-ris Vi-rum, per-fe - ɛti

cor - po-ris, in for - ma no - ſtri ge -

neris

ne-ris.   O Pa-tris mi-ra be - nig-ni-tas!

O ma-tris præ-cel-ſa dig-ni-tas!   Quæ

pro ſa-lu - te ho - mi-num cœ-li Re-

gem' & Do-mi-num ſa-cra - to fo-uet

gre-mi-o;   quem or - di-nes an-ge - li-ci

     laudant

lau-dant, ad- o - rant cœ-li-ci ci-ues in reg-

ni præ-mi-o. O Ma-ri - a, vir-go

pi-a, or-ta di-a ex re - gi-a pro-

ge-ni - e: Ex-pers ma-ris, De-um

pa-ris, por-tum ma-ris, fa-lu - ta-ris

141 ſpem

spem ve-ni-æ.   In cu - ius lau-de de - fi-cit

mens, lin - gua, fen - fus, ra-ti-o,   Sed laus

hæc e - ius re - fi-cit   cœ-le - fti nos

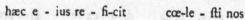

fo-la - ti - o.   Quæ, fo-la præ-bens fo - la-

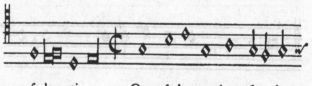

ti - a, eft fcho-la do-cens ve - ra-ci - a.

Scientiam

Sci-en - ti-am cum ar - ti-bus, o-ra - ti-o -

nis par-ti bus, hanc cun-cta lau-dant gram-ma-

ta. Rhe-to - ri-cam cum flo - ri-bus ve-

nu - stis - q co-lo-ri-bus ac Lo - gi-cæ So-phiſ-

ma-ta. Dig-na-re me lau-da-re te, O ſan-ctiſ-

ſima

si-ma do-mi-na. Li-bro fcri-bi vi-tæ ti-bi fac

de-uo-to - rum no-mi-na. Tu Tri-ni-ta-tis

tem-plum, ex-em-plum iu-fti-ci-æ, tu re-na-

tis fan-cti-ta-tis fpe-cu-lum. Ro-fa fi-ne fpi-

na & vi-a mun-di-ci-æ, tu fol lu-ftrans &

illuftrans

il-lu-ſtrans   ſe-cu-lū.   Du-&trix gre-gis, do-
                             Sis in - dul-gens, cla-

&trix le-gis gra-ti-æ, pa-tris ho-nor, car-mē co-
ra ful-gens fa -ci-e, me- i me-mor, cul-pæ pre-

nor   con-de-re.   Sed vi-tı - a, fla-gi-
mor   pon-de-re.

ti - a   tu re-la-xa-re pro-pe-ra,   Ut Do-mi-

no quem no-mı-no, me -a gra-ta ſint o - pe-ra.

Am-bi-ti-o, tra-di-ti-o, fe - di-ti-o, Di-

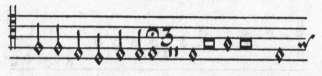

ræ ne vul-nus fau-ci-at.   O-ra De-um, pla-

cans e - um, ne   me re - ŭ in-fer-ni Styx de-

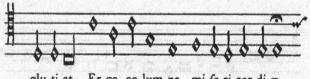

glu-ti-at. Er-go, co-lum-na mi-fe-ri-cor-di-æ,

Pa-cis a - lum-na, ba-fis - q con-cor-di-æ. Me

non

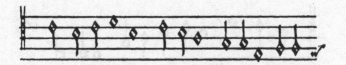

non ob re-a-tum de-fpi-ce; re-fpi-ce pi-e-

ta-tis o-cu-lo. Vir-tu-te be-a-tum ef-fi-ce,

re-fi-ce vi-ui fon-tis po-cu-lo. Ma-ter mi-fe-ri-

cor-di-æ, Spes & fa-lus ve-ni-æ.　Bo-ni-
　　　　　　　　　　　　　　　　　　　 Dat pau-

tas im-men-fa, ple-na De-i gra-ti-a, me Paper a-mi-cus car-men ti-bi mel-li-cum, po-ftu-

　　　　　　　　　　　　　　 tris

tris in men-sa pa-ne vi-tæ sa-ti - a.
lat men - di - cus à te do-num cœ-li -cum.

Sal-ua mul-tis an-nis, sis no-bis pe-ren-nis vi-ta,

ve-ri-tas, vi - a. Ut poſt fi-nem vi-tæ ſor-ti - a-

mur ri-tè ſem-pi-ter-na bra-ui - a. Sit laus De - o

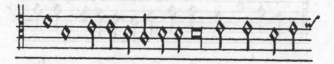

Pa-tri, Na-to-q vi-Eto-ri - a. Per quem ſu - æ

matri

ma-tri mag-na da-tur glo-ri - a. Nos am-bo-rum

pneu-ma e - ri-gat, di-ri-gat, cu-ra re-gat fe-

du-la. Et me-lo-dum neu-ma in-to-net, per-fo-

net per æ - ter-na fe-cu-la.

Laus

LXVII

Aus vir - gi - nis Na - ti
Pa - rens ca - rens o - ri -

ſo - nat cum iu-bi-lo, Fraus cri -
gi - nis con - ta-gi- o, To - tis

mi - nis ab - ſit, cul - pæ fu -
vo - tis te car - mi - nis lau -

ga - to nu-bi-lo. Cœ - tus
dat præ - co-ni-o. Ce - dit

no - ſtri col - le - gi - j. Læ - tus
lu - ctus tri - ſti - ci - æ. Re - dit

fe - sto   na - ta - lis   re - gi - j.
per   te   fru - ctus   iu - sti - ci - æ.

Præ - de - sti - na - ta no-sce-ris in sa -
San - cta   pri - us quàm na-sce-ris in lu -

lu - tem   cre - den - ti-um,   A Pro-
cem   or - ta   gen - ti-um.   Quæ de-

phe-tis   præ-cog - ni - ta sig - no - rum
cre -tis   es præ - di - ta do - no - rum

(b)

æ - nig - ma-ti-bus,   Da - uid
cha - rif - ma-ti-bus.   Vir - go

semen

se - men, ſtirps re-gi - a, vir - ga Ieſ -
pro- les e - gre-gi - a, ſer -uans pu -

ſe flo - ri - ge-ra,
do - ris fœ - de-ra. Tu ſtel-la, quæ bel-

la pro-cel - la - rum de-ſti-tu-is. Ma-ri - a,

ſpem pi - a gra-ti - a - rum re -ſti - tu-is.

Por - ta clau - ſa nec per-ui-
Por - tus ma - ris pe - ri-cu-

a, Or - ta   no - bis   qua lux
lis, Hor - tus   clau - sus   De - j

est   præ-vi - a;   Si - gno   fons   in-de-fi-
fig - na-cu-lis   Re - dun - da - re   suf-fi-

ci-ens   fig - na - tus   fan - cti   Spi-
ci-ens mun - do   flu - en - ta   cœ-

ri-tus.   Au-di nos, dos ho- no-ris, & flos,
li-tus.   Vi-tæ pax, fax a - mo-ris, ve - rax

in - ter flo-rum et ro-fa - rum mil - li - a,
quæ cæ-lo-rum re-gem, na - ti fi - li - a,

tu

tu pri - ma-tum so - lus poſ-ſi-des.
no-bis pla-cas, cui nunc aſ-ſi-des.

Tu es vir-tu-tis nos tra-hens ex - em-plum, in
In ſpe ſa-lu-tis ad te, pa - cis tem-plum, tre-

o - do-rem poſt te cur-ri-mus:
men - tes ab ho - ſte fu-gi-mus.

Cu-ius di - ra ne-qui-ti - a, fal-lax & in - fi -
Vt tan-dem ad ſup-pli-ci - a ſe-cum tra-hat cru-

de-lis, Se-du-xit nos ad vi-ti - a de-cep-ti - o-
de-lis, ab e - ius nos ſæ-vi-ci - a ſem-per tu - e-

num

num te-lis,   O fa- lus ho - mi-num, Cu-
ri ve-lis.   O lu-men lu - mi-num il -

rans̡ nos dex- te -ra,   Tu ru-bus ar-dens cre-
lu-ſtrans æ -the-ra.   Tu ar-cus fa- cri fœ-

de-ris, tu vel-lus Ge-de- o -nis,   Tu cœ-li
de-ris, tu thro-nus Sa- lo-mo-nis.   Ver-bi De-

fan - ¢tu- a -ri- um, tu cla-uis Pa-ra-di-ſi,
j ſa -cra-ri-um à Pa-tre in-di-ui-ſi.

Ex-cel-ſa ſu-pra ſy-de-ra, ti-bi ce-dit   na-tu-ra.

        Nam

Nam te vir-tu-tū o - pe-ra præ - fig-nant in fcrip-

tu - ra.　Tu Iu-dith for-tis, He-fter mor-tis in

ca-put fen-tē-ti - ā con-uer-tens Ha - man pra-

ui.　Tu Su-na-mi-tis, Io-el vi-tis, Si-fa-ris po-

ten-ti-am re-fu-tans ic-tu cla-ui.　O fan-cta
Tu no-ftra
domina

do - mi-na, pre-ca-mur mi - se-ri: Na-to
no - mi-na fac cœ-lis in - se-ri.

com-men-da & e - men-da nos con-si-li - o.   In

hoc dig-na-re gu-ber-na-re nos ex - i - li - o.

A ma-lis   e - ru - e, ad-uer-sa de - stru - e,
Re - a-tum di - lu - e, sa- lu-tem tri - bu - e.

Sta-tum in-no - cu-æ vi-tæ re-sti-tu - e.   Te
Sto- la per-pe - tu-æ pa-cis nos in-du- e.   Quæ

collaudantes

col- lau-dan-tes a-fpi-ce nos, de-cus an-ge-lo-rum,
di -gni- ta -tis a-pi-ce te-nes ar-cem cœ-lo-rum.

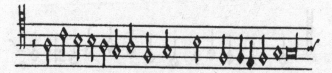

E-ya fo-la-ri fa-ci - e fplen-dens cœ-li re-gi-na,

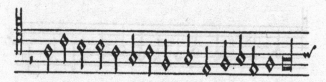

cœ-le-ftis au-la gra-ti - æ, fer-ua nos à ru - i - na.

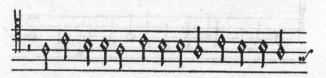

Tu vas vir-tu-tũ, no-bis tu-tum e - fto fcu-tum

mu-ni-ens ab i - ra De - i mag-ni. Tu forma

ma le-gis, ma-ter Re-gis, duc-trix gre-gis, u -

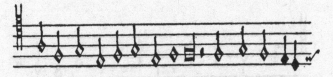

ni-ēs mor-te re-dem-tos ag-ni,   Te cor-dis ſtu-
Vo - cis tri - pu-

di- o ex- o -rat a - ni-mus.   Vt nos con-
di - o me-los hoc ca - ni-mus.

du-cas & ad-du-cas Re-gi Do - mi-no, Qui

reg-nat te-cū & tu ſe-cum ſi-ne ter-mi-no.

       Qui

Qui se de-dit in pre-ci-um no-stræ re-dem-ti - o-

nis, Det quo - q per te præ-mi-um re-mu-ne-

ra-ti - o - nis. Vt con-gau-den-tes & plau-den-

tes iu-gi-ter nos v - ni-ta-ti tri-næ, Lau-des

pan-ga-mus & ca-na-mus dul-ci-ter reg-nan-ti
sine

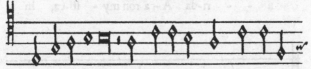

fi-ne fi-ne.   Sit fi-nis hu-ius car-mi-nis, & can-

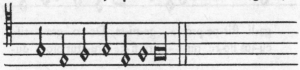

ti - o fi-ni-ta,   quæ di-ci-tur *Laus Vir-gi-nis,*

Chri-fti laus in - fi - ni - ta.

LXVIII

- Ni - ca gra   -   ti - fe - ra le-
Ex Ia-cob fur   -   git ftel - la, mun-

gis ve-te-ris um-bræ fu-ga,   ve - ri - ta-tis lu-
do dum o - re - ris lu - ci-da,   flo-rens vir-gu-la

M   161   cifera,

ci - - fe-ra, Virgo flo-ri - ge-ra, Re-
a - - ri-da A - a-ron my - fti-ca, in

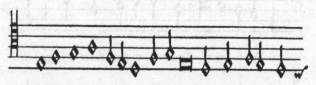

ga-li ftir-pe pro - ge-ni-ta, De-o gra - tif-
cu-ius flo-re mi - ri-fi-cè fru-ctus pro - du-

fi-ma.　　No-uum fig - nū lau-de dig-num
ci-tur.　　In-car-na - ri, mun-do da - ri
　　　　　Dum im-ple - uit quod de-cre - uit,

i - mi-ta-tur mi - ra - bi-le,　　Flo-rum flos,
cœ-lo mi-fit Ver-bum Pa-ter,　　So- la fpes
vi-rū cir-cum-dans mu - li -er.

　　　　　　　virtutum

vir - tu - tum dos, Vir-go ro -ſa for-mo
tu no - bis es Doc-trix mo-rŭ bo-no-

ſa, tu vi - tis fruc-tu - o - ſa, ab-ſint per te do-
rŭ, ſo-la -men pec-ca -to -rum, iu- ua-men mi-ſe-

lo - ſa, abſ-ter-ge vi -ti - a.   Gau-
ro -rum pro no-bis ſup-pli-ca.   Ru-

de,   Ma-ter mi-ra - bi-lis, quæ in ſcrip-tu-
bus   ar-dens non u - ri-tur, dum im-pre-gna-

ris & fi -gu-ris ful-ges ve - ne-ra - bi-lis,
tur, fœ-cun-da-tur pa-rens vi - ri nę -ſci- a,

ſpectabilis

spe-&ta - bi-lis. De mon-te fi - ne ma-
vir-go pi- a. Lig- nū a-quis im-mer-

ni-bus la-pis mi-rè præ-fcin-di-tur, nã de fiſ-
gi-tur, Ma-rath dul-cor in - fū -di-tur, nã ſer-uãs

cel-la à pu-el-la Mo- y- ſes e -du - ci-tur,
ur -na nos di-ur-na pa -ne vi - tæ præ- pa-ra,

vi-tæ da-tur. Ter- ra-rum no-ſtra-rum fons
ſal-ui - fi-ca. Ser-uo-rum tu- o -rum pre-

ri-gans ſu-per-fi - ci-es, ex te no-ſtræ ſa-lu -
ces be-nig-nè ſuſ- ci-pe, ma-ter mi- ſe - ri-cor-

        tis

tis ſpes, vel-ut de pra-tis   vo-lu-pta-tis flu-ui-
di - æ pla-cans i - ra-tum red-de gra-tum no-ſtrum

us e -gre - di-tur, fons læ - di-tur.   Tu
mi - ni-ſte - ri-um de - i - fi-cum.   Por-

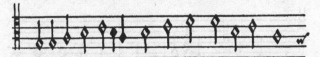

ve-ri Sa-lo-mo — nis e-bur-ne-is [in] thro-
ta E-ze-chi- e   — lis, tu   la -cus Da-ni - e -

nis, ap - ta co-ro-nis hanc ple — be-cu-lam.
lis, ca - ſta, fi -de-lis, tu   mun-di do-mi-na.

Im — plo-rat, qui cog-no-ſcit ſe re-um &
Ab   i -mis ad ſu-per- na, cœ-le-ſte di-

depoſcit

de-po-ſcit per te ſub-li-ma   -   ri.   Cum
a -de-ma o - ra no-bis da   -   ri.

dig-nè de te fa-ri,   te ve-ne-ra-ri   non   va -
Re-ſpi-ce af-fe-ctum, cu-ra de-ſe-ctum, iu - ua-men

-le-o,   Re - ſu-ſci- ta de-preſ-ſum,
præ-ſti-to.   Ab   ho-ſti-bus de-fen -de,

& ob - ti - ne in - greſ- ſum pa - cis in - fi -
pi - um na-tum o - ſten- de poſt hunc fi -nem

ni - tæ.
vi - tæ.

LXIX

PRIMA VOX

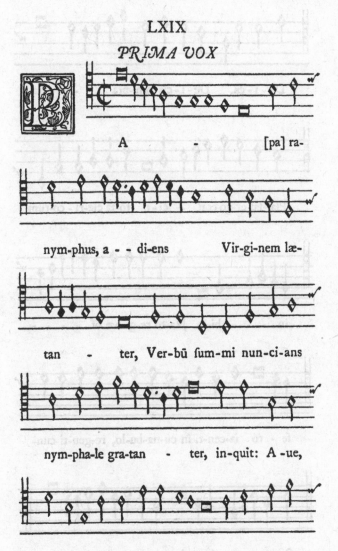

A - [pa] ra-

nym-phus, a - - di-ens Vir-gi-nem læ-

tan - ter, Ver-bū ſum-mi nun-ci-ans

nym-pha-le gra-tan - ter, in-quit: A-ue,

cœ-li-ca vir-go gra-ui-da - ta, ex-tans ma-ter

Deica,

De - i - ca, De - i - cis um-bra - ta.

Pfal-lat er-go con - ci - o to-ta cle-ri - co-rum

iu - - - bi-lo. Na-to re-gi-næ of - - - -

fe - ro ia-cen-ti in cu-na-bu-lo, re-gen-ti cun-

&a ver - bu - lo, ver - - - - bu-lo.

Paranymphus

Pᴀ - [pa] ra-nym-

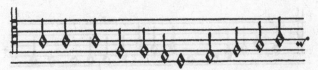

phus, a - di-ens vir-gi-nem læ-tan - ter,

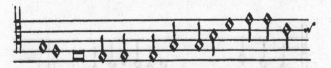

Ver-bum Sum-mi nun-ci-ans nym-pha-le gra-

tan - ter, In-quit: A - ue, cœ-li-ca virgo gra-

ui-da - ta, ex-tans ma-ter De-i-ca, De-i-

cis

cis um-bra - ta. Pſal-lat er-go con - - ci - o

to-ta cle-ri-co-rum iu - - bi - lo. Na-to re-gi-

næ of - fe-ro ia-cen-ti in cu-na-bu-lo, re-gen-

ti cun-cta ver-bu-lo, ver - - - bu-lo.

LXX

PRIMA VOX

Ar - [par]-

ce, vir-go, ſpes re - o - - - rum,

pœ-ni-ten - ti ſer - uu-lo, e - um ſol-uens

à ſu-o - rum de-li-&o-rum vin - cu-lo,

vin-cu-lo. - - - Po-tes e - nim

171

quantum

quan-tum ve - lis: er-go par-ce, do-mi-na,

do - mi-na. Ad quid nam - q te fi-de-

lis, ni-fi fo-rent cri-mi-na, cri-mi-na, in-uo-

ca-ret? nec tu fo - res, fo - res, tan-to dig-na

fi - li - o, fi - li - o,   ni - - - -

[ni] fu-if-fent pec-ca-to-res, & pa-trum tranf-

gref-fi-o, - - - tranf-gref-fi-o. Et-fi

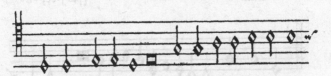

pœ-nam cul-pa pof-cit, cul-på de-le ve-ni - a,

ve - ni - a, cum fit ma-ior quæ ig-no-fcit

quàm is cui fit gra - ci - a, gra - -

cia.

ci - a.

ALTERA VOX

Par - [par]-ce, vir-

go, ſpes re - o - - - rum pœ-ni-

ten-ti ſer - uu-lo, e - um ſol-uens à ſu - o-

rum de - li -Cto-rum vin - cu-lo, vin-cu-

174   lo

lo. - - - Po-tes e - nim quan-

tum ve - lis: er-go par-ce, do-mi-na, do -

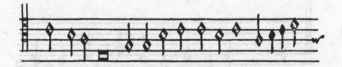

mi-na. Ad quid nam - q̃ te fi-de-lis, ni-ſi fo-

rent cri - mi-na, in-uo-ca-ret? nec tu fo -

res, fo - res tan-to dig-na fi - li - o,

175 filio

fi - li - o,   ni - - - [ni] fu-if-

fent pec - ca - to - res & pa - trum trãf - gref - fi-

o, ij   tranf - gref - fi - o. Et-fi pœ-

nam cul-pa po-fcit, cul-pam de-le ve-ni-a,

ve - ni - a, cum fit ma-ior quæ ig-no-fcit

quã

quã is cui fit gra - ci - a, gra - -

- - - ci - a.

DE FRAGILITATE
& miserijs humanae
conditionis

LXXI

Vnc flo-ret   men-da-ci-um, pra-
Fraus do-nis   co -ro-na-tur, vir-
Tunc vis vir-tu-tis vi -gu- it, dis-

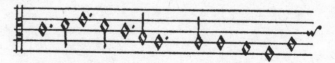

ui- ta -tis con-sor-ti-um;   in mun-do di - li-
tus sub pe- de da - tur;   pi - e -tas & fi-
ci- pu-lus dum ti-mu-it   do- &to - rē cum pu-

gun - tur, qui fal- sa ob - lo -quun - tur:
de - li -tas   est tan-quā be - sti - a - li-tas:
do - re: sed iam ad- di -scunt mo - re

veritas

ve - ri   tas mu-ta-bi-tur,   & fi - des de - fo -
in -di - gnus re - ci-pi-tur,   e - ge-nus ve - rò
ma-la   pro-pa-ga - re,   nec vo-lunt nunc a -

la - bi-tur,   a - ma - bi-tur ne-qui - ti - a,
pre-mi-tur; Mam-mon & u - fu - ra Sa-tha-næ
ma - re   ar - tis   in - cre - men - tum:

di - fper - di-tur iu - fti - ci - a: pra-ua a -
funt cu - ra præ - ci - pu - è: iu - ra re-
fit er -go de - tri -men - tum   præ-fa-tæ

ua - ri - ti - a, iam & va -na glo-ri - a; in cun-
nu-e - runt, iam & bo - na di - ui - fe-runt, ma-
di -fci-pli-næ; mo-res dant ru - i - næ;   fen-

179   ctis

ctis ma-lig- na -tur,   ſi ti -bi ſit iu-ſti- ci - a;
la re -po-nun-tur. Heu ſtu- di -j mo- ra- li - tas,
ſu a -bu-tun-tur.

iam mun — di ſæ-ui-ti - a ma-lĕ te tri - -
ri - go- ris quip-pe bo-ni-tas lap-ſum pa-ti - -

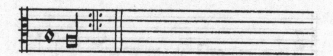

ſta - tur.
un - tur.

LXXII

N   [in] hoc vi-
Con   -   [con] clu - dit
Bel   -   [bel] la mo-
Sur   -   [fur] fum men-

tæ fta   -   di - o di -uer- fa con - di -
in tu   -   mu-lo mors mul-tos ex cu-
uent plu - ri-ma, mun-dus & dæ -mo-
tē e   -   ri-ge, tu - a fa-Eta cor-

ti - o   car-nis eft hu- ma - næ:
mu-lo   po-pu - li fre-quen - ter;
ni - a   car-nem in- fe -ftan - tes:
ri -ge,   in hac vi-ta du - ra,

A   -   [a] -git hic in vi - -
Oc   -   [oc]-cul-tat in pul - -
vul   -   [vul]-nus fuf-fert a - -
la   -   [la] -bi- li ac fla - -

             tijs,

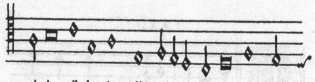

ti -js, il -le in di -ui - ti -js, & hic
ue -re di -ui -tem cum pau - pe - re, tunc in-
ni -ma ex e - if -dem fau - ci - a: cla-mant
bi -li, de -bi - li ac fle - bi -li, ci -tò

e -get pa - ne: mors vt po - nit me-
dif- fe - ren - ter. Fa -ctis vel ver-
hoc gu - ftan - tes. Pa - ce fru - i ple-
tran- fi - tu - ra. Sen -tit ad - huc pro-

tas, fu -bit om -nis fe -xus & æ -tas: Cum
bis, ho -mo fim -plex, vn- de fu -per -bis? Nam
na cu -pi -ens, de for -de re -fre -na car-
les quod com - mi -fê -re pa -ren -tes: Hinc

mors quem -q fe -rit, quis
fi cre -di - - de -ris tu
nem, mor -ti - - fe -ris ne
tu - a fa - cta re -ge, nec

182 [quis]

[quis] mo-dò tu -tus   e -rit?
[tu] ci -tò pul-uis   e -ris.
[ne] pa -re - at vi -   ti - js.
[nec] ma-la cor-de   te - ge.

LXXIII

Am   [iam] ve-rus   a-mor
Iam   [iam] le-gem do-lus

ex- pi -ra-uit,   pax in ter- ris e-xul-a-uit,
im-pug-na-uit,   to-tus mũ-dus ſe mu-ta-uit,

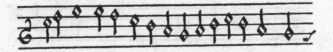

Pa - tri pro-no -   - les
no - ua lex   ex-

imperat.

im - pe - rat. Fi - dem fraus in - car - ce - rat,
su - pe - rat. Om - nes mun - di se - mi - tas

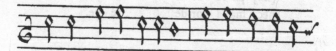

fa - mam lin - gua la - ce - rat, re - gem rex e - xu -
oc - cu - pa - uit no - ui - tas, va - ni - tas, i - ni

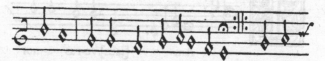

pe - rat, ple - bem plebs vi - tu - pe - rat. Quis er -
qui - tas, guer - ra vel ho - sti - li - tas. E - bri -

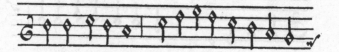

ro - res nu - me - rat quos
a mo - der - ni - tas res

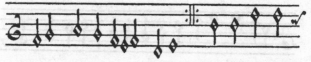

mun - dus ex - ag - ge - rat? Bel - la pla - cent
a - mat in - so - li - tas. Vul - gus ha - bet

aulicis

au - li-cis, pro-ter-ui-re ru - sti-cis,
o - ne-ra, æ-gre fe-rens vul - ne-ra:

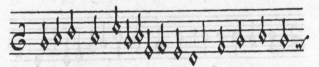

v-su-ra po-li - ti-cis, Si- mo -ni - a
quis ne-scit quot o - pe-ra se-quun-tur post

cle - ri-cis.   Plus pla-cet iam fa-tu- i-tas
fu - ne-ra?   Plus trun-ca-tus ha-bi-tus

quàm per-so-na-rum Tri-ni-tas, plus De-ci-j
quàm do-na sa-ncti Spi-ri-tus, plus i -do-lo-

no - bi-li-tas quàm fi-des, spes, & ca-ri-tas.
rum ser-ui-tus quàm pro pec - ca-tis ge-mi-tus.

Plus

Plus pla-cet cri-nis tra-cti-o quàm Pſal-mus
Iam am-ple-ctun-tur o-di-o cle - rus

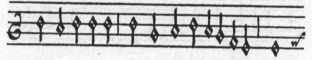

vel o-ra-ti-o, plus ve-ne-ris a-bu-ſi-o quàm
& Re-li-gi-o. Quis no-uit ab i-ni-ti-o tot

miſ-ſa vel de-uo-ti-o. Ma - ior
ri-uu-los à vi-ti-o? Pœ - na

ce-dit & o-be-dit; mi-nor ſe-nem ar - - -
ia-cet, cul-pa pla-cet cle-ris, ſer-uis, do - - -

gu-it; ſchiſ-ma re-dit, re-tro-ce-dit lex
mi-nis: do-cti de-gunt, ſtul-ti re-gunt, lu-

quæ

quæ pri-us pla - cu-it.   Pom-pa pla-cet
cra dan-tur a - si-nis.

fœ - mi - nis, ta - lis sta-tus ho - mi - nis eſt in

mun - di ter - mi - nis.

LXXIV
TENOR

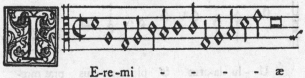

E-re-mi - - - - - - - æ
Nam Ra-che - - - - - - lis
Fraus He-ro - - - - - dis
Pœ - na ia - - - - - cet,

187   prophetiæ

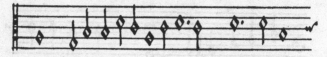

pro - phe - ti   —   —   æ fty -lus
gens cru -de   —   —   lis na -tum
pra - uis mo   —   —   dis to -ti
cul - pa pla   —   —   cet, cle-ris,

no -vè   pin-gi -tur,   Hie-rar-chi - æ ma-
fu -dat fter-ne - re;   ven-tis, ve - lis, frau-
ter-ræ   im -pe -rat,   fi -dem fran-gat, ca -
fer-uis,   do -mi -nis: Iu - fti de -gunt, ftul-

tris pi - æ vox in Ra   —   ma gig-ni -tur:
dis te - lis quof- q vult   pe - ri -me - re.
ptus plã -gat, no - ua lex   ex - u -pe - rat.
ti re -gunt cũ -ctis mun   —   di ter-mi -nis.

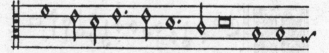

U -lu -la- tus   & plo - ra- tus   præ mœ-
Nunc rap-to-rum   ex - a -cto-rum   qui pla-
Ma -ior ce- dit   & o - be- dit,   mi - nor
Con -cul-ca- tur,   e -ner - ua - tur   cle - rus

         rore

ro - re fi - li - æ. Nam af -
cent in cu - ri - a, Do - mi -
se - nem ar - gu - it, Schi - ſma
& re - li - gi - o. Quiſ - nam

fa - - tus nec ſo - - - la - tus
no - - rum op-preſ - - - ſo - rum
re - - dit, re - tro - - ce - dit
ſci - - uit, vel au - - di - uit

hanc vir eſt cle - men - ti - æ.
tol-lunt res cum fu - ri - a.
lex, quæ pri - us pla - cu - it.
tot ri - uos à vi - ti - o?

BASSVS

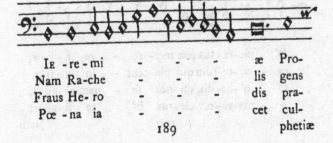

Ie - re - mi - - - æ Pro-
Nam Ra-che - - - lis gens
Fraus He- ro - - - dis pra-
Pœ - na ia - - - cet cul-

phetiæ

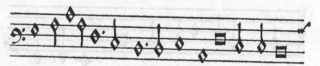

phe- ti   –   –   æ ſty- lus no- vè pin- gi-tur,
cru- de   –   –   lis na-tum ſu-dat ſter-ne-re:
uis mo   –   –   dis to- ti ter-ræ im-pe-rat,
pa pla   –   –   cet cle- ris, ſer-uis, do -mi-nis,

Hie - rar - chi - æ ma - tris pi - æ
ven - tis, ve - lis, frau - dis te - lis
fi - dem fran - git, cap - tus plan - git,
Iu - ſti de - gunt, ſtul - ti re - gunt

vox in Ra - ma gig- ni -tur: U -lu-la-tus
quoſ- q̄ vult pe - ri- me- re. Nunc rap-to-rū,
no -ua lex ex- u -pe-rat, Ma -ior ce-dit
cunc-tis mun - di ter- mi-nis, Con -cul-ca-tur,

& plo-ra- tus præ mœ- ro - re fi -li -æ,
ex - ac -to-rum qui pla-cent - in cu- ri-a,
& o -be- dit, mi-nor ſe - nem ar-gu-it,
e - ner-va- tur cle -rus & re - li-gi -o:

190   Nam

Nam af -fa - - tus nec fo - - -
Do - mi -no - - rum op-pref - - -
Schi-fma re - - dit, re-tro - - -
quif -nam fci - - uit vel au - - -

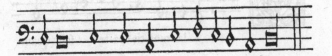

la- tus Hanc vir eft cle - men - ti - æ.
fo- rum tol -lunt res cum fu - ri - a.
ce- dit lex, quæ pri - us pla - cu- it.
di- uit tot ri -uos à vi - ti- o?

De

DE VITA SCHO-
LASTICA

LXXV

L-la mor-tis pa-te - scit quam

vi-dit Ihe-re - mi - - - - - as:

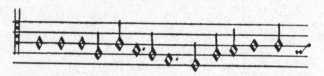

Cle-ri sta-tus vi-le - scit sper-nen - do Scho-

læ vi - - - - as. Scho-la,

nola

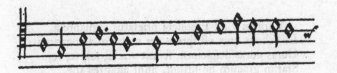

no-la vir-tu - tis, tu-tis clan-ge - scit mo -

ri-bus: qui sper-nunt, cer-nunt luc - tum;

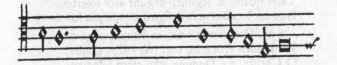

fruc-tum per-dunt cum

flo - ri - bus.

L inquunt Scholas Scholares, iam spreta disciplina,
Doctis apparent pares, parua docti doctrina,
Artes, partes postponunt, præponunt aulizare:
Qui scit parum quid scribere, ære se vult ditare.

A postata infestus, vt suos plus molestat,
Aulæ scriptor molestus sic & clerum infestat,
At cura prælatura aulizantes exaltat;
Prouectos, vita rectos, hos honor iam persaltat.

V irgam vidit Propheta præfatus vigilantem,
In Scholis quæ eſt ſpreta per mentem arrogantem;
Curas duras deſpiciunt, ſciunt vix la, ſol, fa, re,
Statim gradum ſic ſitiunt, fiunt aſtantes aræ.

V itæ via vitatur, dùm clero deuiatur;
Pro libris trupha datur, taxillis diſputatur.
Tales quales hi regunt; degunt arte ſolertes.
Heu lex! quàm grex inſignis dignis præfert inertes!

S ors Dei extat clerus, ex Scholis procreatus,
Vt ſit votis ſyncerus, orat pro vulgo gratus:
O Chriſte, pie Domine, eſto clero ſolamen,
Vt hi, qui tibi militant, vitent dirum examen.

ACROSTICON, OLAVVS.

LXXVI
PRIMA VOX

E - - - - [re]-

gi-men ſcho-la - - ri-um vo-lo com-

men-da - re, ſpe - ro nec con-tra -

rium

ri-um mi-hi ob-ui - a - re, mo-dò nam ſcho-

la-res non ſunt pa - res, ex o - lim pro-uec - tis

ſub-iec - - tis. Eſt & in me-mo -

ri - a, taŋ-quã in mar-mo-re - a ta-bu-la de-

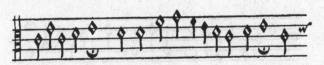

pic - ta. In-ter mil-le mi - li-a non
tàm

tàm pul-chra fi - - li - a, vt me-a præ-

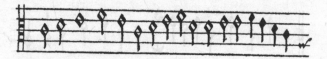

dic - ta, tan-to non - - - -

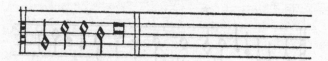

ag-mi-ne vic-ta.

ALTERA VOX

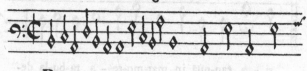

RE - - - - - [re]-gi-men Scho-

la - - ri-um vo-lo com-men-da - re,

fpero

fpe-ro nec con-tra - ri-um mi-hi ob-ui - a -

re; mo-dò nam Scho-la-res non funt pa - res

ex o-lim pro-uec - tis fub-iec - tis. Eft &

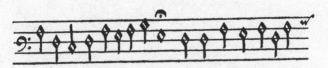

in me-mo - ri - a, tan-quã in mar-mo-re - a

ta-bu-la de-pic - ta. In-ter mil-le mi - lia,

197

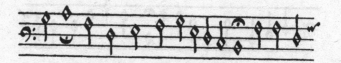

li - a, non tàm pul-chra fi - li - a, vt me - a

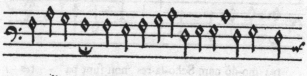

præ-dic - ta, tan-to non - - - ag-

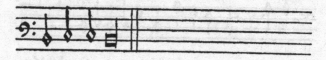

mi - ne vic - ta.

HISTORICA
Cantio

LXXVII

A - - - mus vi - rens o - li-
Bi - - - num ge - nus a - ni-

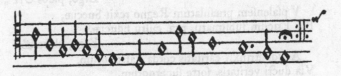

ua - - - rum per co-lum - bam pan-di-tur;
ma - - - rum ar - ca No-ẽ clau-di-tur.

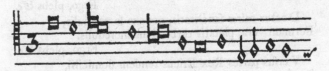

Er-go, plebs Fin-no - ni-ca, gau-de de hoc

do - no, quòd fac - ta es Ca - tho-li-ca

Verbi

Ver-bi De - i ſo - no.

Apex montis abſcondatur, aquæ vis dùm tollitur,
Nubis ſordes expurgatur, ſignum rei ponitur.

      Ergo, plebs &c.

Grande mirùm, pietatis arca dùm ſaluatur,
At tunc cunctis animatis ira Dei datur.

      Ergo, plebs &c.

Velut noſtro demonſtratur doctore Finlandiæ,
Fides Chriſti dùm fundatur, linquenti terrâ Angliæ.

      Ergo, plebs &c.

Vpſalenſem præſulatum Regno rexit Sueciæ,
Per Ericum ſublimatũ, præ cultu fiduciæ.

      Ergo, plebs &c.

Ardor ſtrinxit caritatis corda Patronorum,
Via ducti veritatis, ſorte ſupernorum.

      Ergo, plebs &c.

Læti petunt Finnonum terram peruenire,
Cultum pellunt Dæmonum, palmam reperiêre.

      Ergo, plebs &c.

Doctor miræ ſanctitatis, ponens ſe periculis,
Formam veræ pietatis turbis dans incredulis.

      Ergo, plebs &c.

Verſus partes Rex Ericus tendens domicilij,
Sanctus præſul hic Henricus comes fit exilij.

      Ergo, plebs &c.

Subit pœnas patienter palmam per martyrij,
Adeſt lictor vehementer potũ dans exitij.

      Ergo, plebs &c.

Chriſtus nobis Patrẽ oret, pacem ſeruans patriæ,
Laudis turba quem decoret, firma fide variè.

      Ergo, plebs &c.

ACROSTICON, *RAGVVALDVS*

          De

DE NATIVITATE

LXXVIII

Ag-nũ no-men Do-mi-ni E - ma-

nu-el, quod an-nun-ci - a - tum eſt per Ga-bri-el.

Ho-di - e ap-pa-ru-it, ap-pa-ru-it in Iſ-ra-el,

ex Ma-ri - a vir-gi-ne eſt na-tus Rex.

FINIS

EXPLANATORY NOTES

Explanatory Notes

I. ANGELVS EMITTITVR. ¶ The Text: of uncertain date and origin. Firſt appearance, ſo far as is at preſent known, in PIÆ CANTIONES (1582). Reprinted by Klemming (1886), II, p. 12, and thence copied by Dreves, vol. XLV*b*, No. 170, p. 136, of his 'Analecta Hymnica.' ¶ The Tune: in the Dorian and Hypo-Dorian modes. Set to the Swediſh words, *Gudh vthſende Engel ſin*, it reappears in Rhezelius' 'Någre Pſalme' (1619), p. 35. In 1853, in free imitation of Petri's words, Neale publiſhed his *Gabriel's meſſage does away*. See 'Carols for Chriſtmas-tide,' No. iii, and 'The Cowley Carol Book' (1902), No. 8.

II. IN HOC ANNI CIRCVLO, with its refrain VERBVM CARO FACTVM EST. ¶ The earlieſt known form is given by E. Du Méril in his 'Poéſies inédites du Moyen Age' (1854), p. 337. It occurs in a MS. in handwriting of the twelfth century, in the Bibl. Nat., Paris (Lat. 1139, f. 48), partly in the Latin tongue and partly in Provençal. Over and above the information given by Julian in his 'Dict. of Hymnology' (1907), p. 1216 (ii) under *Verbum caro factum eſt*, *q.v.*, it may be added that Dreves diſcovered it in a MS. of the thirteenth century, the 'Antiphonarium Bobbienſe' (Cod. Taurinen. F 1 14); see 'Anal. Hymnica,' XX, p. 22. ¶ In the preface to Neale and Helmore's 'Carols for Chriſtmas-tide' (1853), it is ſtated to be 'one of the moſt popular of Chriſtmas carols, and is found with greater variations than almoſt any other. There is ſcarcely an European language which has not had an ancient tranſlation.' In Germany it appears in the vernacular as *Czu dieſem newen jare tzart*, as *In des jares zirclikait*, or as *Mit dieſem nuwen jare*. ¶ For an Engliſh tranſlation, ſee Neale's 'Medieval Hymns' (1851), p. 74; and for words

205

in

in free imitation of the Latin, see 'Carols for Christmas-
tide' (1853), No. viii. In both cases Neale's carols begin
alike *In the ending of the year*. ¶ The Melody is in the
Dorian mode. For an earlier form of the PIÆ CANTIONES
tune, taken from the Hussite 'Kantional von Jistebnicz,'
circa 1420, and there arranged for two voices, see 'Anal.
Hymnica,' XXIII, Anhang, p. 198. This Jistebnicz form of
the air, in four-part harmony, is to be found as No. 13 in
'The Cowley Carol Book.' ¶ When 'Carols for Christmas and Easter-tide' first appeared in 1853-4, the rule as to
the interpretation of the 'ligature' was not so clearly under-
stood as now. Consequently, not only in the case of *In hoc
anni circulo*, but in many other instances also, the tunes of
PIÆ CANTIONES have been, unintentionally, but nevertheless
incorrectly transcribed in Neale and Helmore's otherwise
admirable work.

III. RESONET IN LAVDIBVS. ¶ Of the fourteenth century.
Often followed by MAGNVM NOMEN DOMINI, see *Cantio* No.
LXXVIII, though the latter may be regarded as complete in
itself. Wicel's 'Psalter Ecclesiasticus' (1550) refers to this
Carol (in the vernacular *Zion sampt den gleubigen*) as one of
the chief 'Jubelgesänge der heiligen Weihnachten, wie
sie unsern Christlichen Vorfaren frölich gesungen.' The
list includes *Der tag der ist so freudenreich* (*Dies est leticie*);
Ein kindelein so löbelich; Es ist das kind zu Bethlehem (*Puer
natus in Bethlehem*); and *In dulci iubilo*. ¶ According to
'Anal. Hymnica,' XX, p. 23, the oldest known form of *Resonet cum laudibus* is contained in the 'Mosburg Gradual'
of the year 1360 (Cod. Univ. Monacen. 157). Wackernagel,
II, No. 605, quotes the old German carol, *Joseph, liber neve
myn*, from a Leipzig MS., No. 1305, of the end of the fourteenth or beginning of the fifteenth century, which was
sung to this melody alternately with *Sunt impleta* and *Magnum
nomen Domini*. Hoffmann von Fallersleben quotes it from
another MS. at München of 1422. It occurs in several
other fifteenth century MSS., and in sixteenth and seventeenth century printed books, Catholick and Lutheran, such
as Spangenberg (1544), Babst (1545), Leisentrit (1567), and
in 'Schöne alte Chatolische Gesang und Ruff,' Tegernsee
(1577); for a list of which see Meister, I, Nos. 27 and 28,

and

and Bäumker, I, pp. 301-6. In more modern works it is to be found in Daniel, I, p. 327, and IV, p. 252. See alfo Wackernagel, I, Nos. 348-354, Kehrein, I, Nos. 94, 96, 125, and 126; befides the collections enumerated in Chevalier's 'Repertorium Hymnologicum,' vol. II, p. 467. Other information may be gleaned from Julian (1907), p. 1668 (i), under the heading *Magnum nomen Domini*, but efpecially from Franz Magnus Böhme's 'Altdeutfches Liederbuch' (1877), No. 521 *a* and *b*. ❡ *Jofeph liber neve myn, hilf mir wygen myn kindelin*, with the anfwer, *Gerne libe mume myn ich helf dir wygen din kindelin*, is known as Maria's 'Wiegenlied,' or 'Cradle Song,' for various readings of which, and for rubrics concerning its manner of finging, the ftudent is referred to Wackernagel, II, Nos. 605-610. ❡ Numerous tranflations or parodies of *Refonet cum laudibus* and *Magnum nomen Domini* are to be found in German facred fong-books, fuch as *Singen wir mit frölichkeit; Zion fampt den gleubigen; Wir loben all' das Kindelein; En natus eft Emanuel; Uns ift ein Kindlein heut' geborn; Es mufz erklingen überall; Singt ihr lieben Chriften all; Grofz und Herr ift Gottes Nam; Do Gabriel der Engel klar*—all teftifying to the immenfe popularity of this fourteenth century melody. ❡ Neale's well-known carol, *Chrift was born on Chriftmas Day* is not a clofe tranflation, but rather a free imitation of *Refonet in laudibus*. See 'Carols for Chriftmas-tide' (1853), No. iv; and 'The Cowley Carol Book' (1902), No. 4. ❡ The Tune, at firft probably Mixo-Lydian, came to be treated, in procefs of time, as a Lydian, and laftly as an Ionian mode melody. In flightly varying form, it may be found in moft of the fixteenth and feventeenth century *Gefangbücher*; and in later books it occurs in Zahn, Nos. 20 and 8573, as well as in Layriz, Meifter (Bäumker), and Böhme. ❡ Bäumker, II, p. 283, remarks on the fimilarity between the fourteenth century tune of *Refonet cum laudibus* and Philipp Nicolai's much admired *Wie fchön leuchtet der Morgenftern* (1599). ❡ The Melody has been often harmonized (for four, five, fix, feven, or eight voices), amongft others, by the following muficians:

(i) Joh. Walther (1544), No. xlvii; (1551), No. li, à 5. See Winterfeld, I, Tonfätze, No. ii; and Michael Prætorius, 'Mus. Sion.,' V (1607), No. lxxxvii, to the words *Jofeph lieber Jofeph mein*.

Leonhart

(ii) Leonhart Schröter (*circa* 1580), for four and eight
voices. See Winterfeld, I, p. 342.

(iii) Samuel Mareſchall, or Lucas Oſiander,[1] as No. 3 in
the latter's 'Funfttzig Geiſtliche Lieder und Pſalmen' (1586); *teſte* Winterfeld, I, p. 471.

(iv) Seth Calviſius (1556-1615) in E. Bodenſchatz' 'Flo-
rilegium Portenſe' (1618), No. lxxxix, a ſix-part
ſetting.

(v) Joh. Andreas Herbſt (1588-1666); *ibid.* p. 25.

(vi) Michael Prætorius' 'Muſæ Sion.,' V (1607), as *Joſeph,
lieber Joſeph mein,* No. lxxxvii, à 5 (already mentioned); and again in the ſame vol., as No. xc, ſet
to the words *Magnum nomen Domini* [*mit vier Tenor-
iſten*]; and again, as No. xci, as *Reſonet in laudibus,*
and *Singt ir lieben Chriſten all,* à 5.

'Muſæ Sion.,' VI (1609), as Nos. xlvi, xlvii, xlviii,
and liv, to the words *Magnum nomen Domini; En
natus eſt Emanuel,* and *Uns iſt ein Kindlein heut' geborn,* à 4.

(vij) Hieronymus Prætorius (1560-1629). A ſetting for
eight voices occurs after his *Magnificat* of the Fifth
Tone (1622). Reprinted in Breitkopf and Haertel's
'Denkmaeler,' Band XXIII, p. 139.

IV. Psallat scholarvm concio. ❡ Peculiar to Piæ
Cantiones. Text reprinted by Klemming, II, p. 45, and
thence embodied in 'Anal. Hymnica,' XLV*b*, No. 165,
p. 134. ❡ In 1853, Neale publiſhed his Carol for Chriſtmas Eve, *Toll! toll! becauſe there ends to-night.* ❡ For two
four-part ſettings of the tune, ſee 'Songs of Syon' (1910),
No. 19; where, to make the Engliſh words to tally exactly
with the Latin, and to agree with the Piæ Cantiones tune,
the pardonable liberty has been taken of inſerting one extra
trochee in the laſt line of every ſtanza. ❡ The Melody, in

---

[1] Although Matthæus Le Maiſtre (1566) and David Wolkenſtein
(1583) ſometimes ſet the Plainſong in the higheſt part, Lucas Oſiander
(1534-1604) was the firſt to entruſt the chief melody ſyſtematically to the
upper voice. Hitherto it had been given to the tenor. See Winterfeld,
I, p. 30, on early three, four, and five-part ſettings of the ſixteenth and
ſeventeenth century; Zahn, VI, No. 260, p. 73; and R. Eitner's 'Quellen-lexikon,' IX, p. 75.

Piæ Cantiones, is written in the Dorian mode, tranſpoſed; but in the fifth line it ſoars a minor third beyond the limits of that ſcale.

V. Personent hodie. ❡ The Text is reprinted in Klemming, II, p. 40, and thence it was drafted into 'Anal. Hymnica,' XLV*b*, No. 167, p. 135. Apparently the parody of an older *Cantio* of four ſtanzas, in honour of St. Nicolas, the words and tunes of which are printed below, beginning *Intonent hodie voces ecclesiæ*.[1] ❡ In Rhezelius' 'Någre Pſalmer' (1619), p. 51, tranſlated into Swediſh, it appears as *Gladheligh ſiunge wij*, ſet to our Piæ Cantiones melody. ❡ In 1854, in his 'Carols for

[1]   Modus i.

In - to - nent ho - di - e   vo - ces ec - cle - ſi - e,

di - es le - ti - ci - e   re - ful - fit   in   mun - do,

er - go le - ta - bun - do   cor - de   iu - bi - le - mus

et   o - re   iu - cun - do.

2. Sanctus hic inclitus | domino ſubditus | in cunis poſitus | vbera vitabat | corpus macerabat | et ter in ſabbato | puer ieiunabat.

3. Parenti miſero | ſubmerſo puero | mari peſtifero | dedit quod petiuit | preces exaudiuit | ſubmerſum puerum | patris cuſtodiuit.

4. Tribus virginibus | victu carentibus | . . . | reddidit honorem | ſubtraxit errorem | reddens virginibus | virgineum florem.

The Words of the above are taken from 'Anal. Hymnica,' XXI, No. 128, p. 86. The Tune from XX (of the ſame work), No. xxii, Anhang, p. 255. The Words and Tune alike are copied by Dreves from the 'Moſburg Gradual' (Cod. Univ. Monacen. 157) of the year 1360.

Easter-tide,' No. xxi, Neale publiſhed his *Let the ſong be begun*, like ſo many of his verſes, compoſed eſpecially for ſome one or other of theſe Piæ Cantiones airs. See alſo 'The Cowley Carol Book' (1902), No. 56. ❡ The Melody is in the Dorian mode, and is remarkable for its ſpirited rhythm. Through an error on the part of one of Auguſtin Ferber's compoſitors, at the beginning of the muſic on page 7 of this volume, there is a ſyllable wanting. *Vir* ſhould be repeated thrice, not twice, on the note A. This omiſſion was already ſuſpected, but is now confirmed by Dreve's *Intonent hodie*, the muſic of which, in the ſixth line of the third ſtanza, requires it to be ſung thus, 'Submerſúm, ſum, ſum, | ſubmerſúm, ſum, *ſum* | ſubmerſúm puerum | patris cuſtodiuit.' See 'Anal. Hymnica,' XXI, No. 128, p. 86.

VI. In dvlci ivbilo. ❡ 'Uff den heyligen Chriſtag.' 'Ein alt Weyhnacht Lied.' A 'Macaronic,' *i.e.* 'Hybrid,' or 'Miſchlied';[1] in this caſe partly in Latin, partly in Swediſh. For many German verſions of this deſervedly favourite Chriſtmas Carol, ſee Kehrein's 'Katholiſche Kirchenlieder' (1859), I, No. 108; Wackernagel, II, Nos. 640-647; and F. M. Böhme's 'Alt deutſches Liederbuch,' No. 528, *a* and *b*. The oldeſt form of the German words is quoted by Wackernagel and Böhme from Codex No. 1305 in the Univerſity Libr. at Leipzig, a MS. of the end of the fourteenth or beginning of the fifteenth century :

1. In dulci iubilo
ſinget und ſit vro.
Aller unſer wonne
layt in preſepio,
Sy leuchtet vor dy ſonne
matris in gremio
qui alpha eſt & o.

2. O Jheſu paruule
noch dir iſt mir ſo we :
troſte mir myn gemute
O puer optime,
durch aller iuncfrawen gute
princeps glorie,
trahe me poſt te.

3. Ubi ſunt gaudia?
nyndert me wen da,
do dy vogelin ſingen
noua cantica,
und do dy ſchelchen klingen
in regis curia
Eya qualia.

4. Mater et filia
iſt iuncfraw Maria
Wir woren gar vertorben
per noſtra crimina
Nu het ſy uns erworben
celorum gaudia
O quanta gracia.

[1] Said by Hoffmann von Fallerſleben in Meiſter, I, No. 24, p. 179, to be the oldeſt example of a ſacred 'mixed' ſong. The Council of Baſel

Another MS. of the fifteenth century at Breſlau varies
the fourth ſtanza thus:

> Mater et filia
> O iungfrau Maria:
> hetteſt du uns nicht erworben
> Celorum gaudia
> So wär wir all verdorben
> per noſtra crimina
> quanta gratia.

Kehrein reads . . . 'wir weren gar verloren | per noſtra
crimina | So haſtu uns erworben | celorum gaudia | Maria
hilff uns da!'

Luther altered this ſtanza, firſt in Babſt's Geſangbuch
(1545), I, No. 56, into 'O patris charitas | O nati lenitas |
wir weren all verloren | per noſtra crimina | ſo hat er uns
erworben | celorum gaudia | Eya, wer wir da!'

¶ The number of Catholick, Lutheran and Bohemian
hymnbooks in which *In dulci iubilo* occurs, in one of its
older forms, or ſet to the more modern words, *In einem ſuſzen
Ton, Lob Gott, du Chriſtenheit,* and *Mit einem ſuſſen Schall,* is
too great to be counted. ¶ For a long time the compoſition
of *In dulci iubilo,* as well as of *Puer natus in Bethlehem,* was
attributed to Peter Faulfiſch, a native of Dreſden, living at
Prag, a friend of Johann Hus, *circa* 1412. But it is certainly
of earlier date. Any doubts as to its authorſhip ſeem to be
removed by a paſſage from Melchior Diepenbrock's 'Heinrich Suſo's' [genannt Amandus] 'Leben und Schriften'
(Regensburg, 1829), quoted by Meiſter, I, No. 24, p. 179.
It may be ſafely conſidered the work of Heinrich Suſo, the
myſtic, the friend of Ioh. Tauler, of the family of the
Counts of Mons, a Dominican Monk, who was born *c.* 1280,
and died in 1365. A paſſage occurring in a MS. of the
fourteenth century, quoted by Diepenbrock, p. 19, quite
decides the matter. The writer recounts 'Wie eines Tages
zu Suſo himmliſche Jünglinge kamen, ihm in ſeinen Leiden
eine Freude zu machen; ſie zogen den Diener[1] bei den
Hand an den Tanz, und der eine Jüngling fing an ein
frohlickes Geſänglein von dem Kindlein Jeſus, das ſpricht

(1431) forbad the uſe in Church of hybrid Cantiones ſuch as 'Ein
verbum bonum et ſuäve' (ſee Neale's preface to 'Sequentiæ ex Miſſalibus').

[1] *I.e.* the ſervant, *i.e.* himſelf.

alſo:

also: IN DVLCI IVBILO,' &c. Like St. Dunſtan and his Miſſa *Rex ſplendens*, we may well believe, that Beatus Suſo learnt his *In dulci iubilo* not of man, but of an angel from heaven. ❡ There is a ſtriking ſimilarity between ſtanza iv of *In dulci iubilo*, and the following beautiful extract from Suſo's writings (ſee Diepenbrock, p. 233), concerning this *Mater et filia*: 'Ach ſüſze Königin, wie billig mag ſich dein frohlicker Name [Geſchlecht] freuen ; denn verflucht war die erſte Eva, daſz ſie der Frucht je entbiſz ; geſegnet ſey die andra Eva, das ſie uns die ſüſze himmliſche Frucht je gebracht! Niemand klage mehr das Paradies ; *wir haben ein Paradies verloren, und haben zween Paradieſe gewonnen*. Oder iſt ſie nicht ein Paradies, in der da wuchs die Frucht des lebenden Baumes, in der alle Wolluſt und Freude mit einander beſchloſſen war ?'

❡ For this melody, in 1853 Neale wrote his *Good Chriſtian men, rejoice*; ſee 'Carols for Chriſtmas-tide,' No. vi. Like that of *Reſonet in laudibus*, the melody, now treated frankly as Ionian, was probably originally in the Mixo-Lydian Mode. For varying forms of the tune ſee Meiſter, I, No. 24; Böhme, No. 528 *a* and *b*; and Zahn, 4947, beſides any of the following collections of muſic where *In dulci iubilo* has been harmonized, for voice or organ, by ſome of the maſter muſicians of every ſucceeding age and generation.

(i) Georg Rhau's (1488-1548) 'Newe Deudſche Geiſt-
    liche Geſenge' (Wittemberg), 1544 : ſee Breitkopf
    and Haertel's 'Denkmaeler' (1908), Bd. XXXIV,
    No. ix, p. 6; à 4, Anon. ſetting; melody in Tenor.
(ii) Joh. Eccard (1533-1611): 'Fünfſtimmige Tonſatze'
    (1597), No. cxx.
(iii) Lucas Oſiander (1534-1604), No. 6: à 4 (1586);
    (?) Samuel Mareſchall (1554-1640).
(iv) Leonard Schröter, *circa* 1572 : for 2 Quires.
(v) Seth Calviſius' 'Harmonia Cantionum Eccleſiaſticarum'
    (1556-1615), No. x (1598), à 4.
(vi) Barth. Geſius' 'Geiſtliche deutſche Lieder' (1601);
    p. 16, à 4.
(vii) Joachim Decker (†1611); No. xli, p. 202 of Gab.
    Huſduvius' 'Melodeyen GB.' 1604 ; à 4.
(viii) Gothardus Erythræus (1608), No. xxix; à 4.
(ix) Melchior Vulpius (1560-1616), No. xv (1609).

Michael

(x) Michael Prætorius (1572-1621), 'Musæ Sioniæ' (1607, Jehnæ), Ander Theil, No. v, for Double Quire. 'Musæ Sioniæ' (1607), V, No. lxxx, à 2; No. lxxxi, à 3; No. lxxxii, à 4; No. lxxxiii, à 4. 'Musæ Sioniæ' (1609), VI, Nos. xxviii and xxix; No. xxxi (Schw. Fran.); No. xxxii (Marck.); No. xxxiii (Preuss. Seest.), all à 4. 'Polyhymnia Panegyrica' (Wolfenbüttel, 1618-9), No. xxiv, for several Quires 'cum tubis,' etc. For a 5 part setting (1597) from 'Mus. Sion.,' VI, No. clxi, see Winterfeld, I, M.-B., No. 120, p. 116.

(xi) Hieronymus Prætorius (1560-1629) in his Magnificat of the 5th Tone, Hamburg (1622), see Breitkopf's 'Denkmaeler,' XXIII, p. 143; à 8.

(xii) Heinrich Grimm (†1637) in Joh. Dillinger's 'Newes Geist. Musikalisch Lustgärtlein' (1626), No. xviii, à 3.

(xiii) Joh. Hermann Schein (1586-1630), 'Cantional' (1627), No. xii, à 4.

(xiv) Samuel Scheidt (1587-1654), in his 'Achtstimmige Geist. Gesänge,' No. xv. [Winterfeld, II, p. 612.]

(xv) Joh. Crüger (1598-1662), No. 98 (1656), 'Praxis pietatis melica,' No. iii. Melody and fig. bass harmonized by Jacob Hintze (1622-1702): No. xlv in his 'Geistliche Kirchen Lieder.'

(xvi) Dietrich Buxtehude (1637-1707). Breitkopf, Bd. II, Part 2, No. 16. 'Orgel Compositionen.' See also Two-choral-preludes, ed. J. E. West (Organ). Novello, 1904.

(xvii) Gottfried Vopelius (1645-1715); 'Neu Leipziger Gesangbuch' (1682), p. 39.

(xviii) Friedr. Wilh. Zachau (1663-1712). Breitkopf, 'Denkmaeler,' Bde. XXI, XXII, p. 353, No. 30. Organ Fugue in G.

(xix) Joh. Gottfried Walther (1684-1748). Breitkopf, Bde. XXVI-XXVII (set as a Choralvorspiel à Clav. et ped.), No. 52, p. 126.

(xx) It is said to have appeared in Scotland, in the 'Gude and Godly Ballates' (1568).

(xxi) 'Lyra Davidica' (1708), p. 7, treble and bass.

(xxii) Joh. Seb. Bach (1685-1750). For Vocal Harmonies see No. 143 of Bach's '371 Vierstimmige Choral Gesänge'

Gesänge' (Breitkopf and Haertel), set to Latin and English words (i) 'The Cowley Carol Book' (1902), No. 12A, and (ii) in 'The Oxford Hymnal' (1909), No. 64. ¶ *In dulci iubilo* is to be found frequently in Bach's Organ Works: Band VII (Breitkopf), No. 29 (Canon in the 8ve.) ; 'Orgel büchlein,' p. 12 ; Bach's 'Werke für Orgel,' No. 106 ; Band VIII (Breitkopf), No. 106, p. 109 ; 'Bach Gesellschaft,' Band IV, Orgelwerke, p. 74, and again at p. 158 ; Choral Vorspiel, Org. 978, 1166, 25 ; and p. 12 ; 40, p. 74 ; Choral (variante) Org. 1217, No. 40, p. 158 ; 'Bach Gesellschaft' (1889), No. 115.

(xxiii) R. L. de Pearsall (1795-1856). See Novello's 'Part Song Book,' Second Series, and No. 16 in 'Kath. GB.' St. Gallen (1863).

(xxiv) Layriz (1855), No. 238.

(xxv) Hauschoralbuch (1887), No. 20. (M. Prætorius, 1607).

VII. Ecce novvm gavdivm. ¶ Reprinted by Klemming, II, p. 22 ; 'Anal. Hymnica,' XLV*b*, No. 162, p. 131. Origin and date unknown. ¶ Neale's *Here is joy for every age* was suggested by this *Cantio* and expressly written for this tune. See 'Carols for Christmas-tide,' No. 1 ; and No. 30 in 'The Cowley Carol Book.' ¶ An eighth mode or Hypo-Mixo-Lydian air. Observe the flat seventh.

VIII. Omnis mvndvs ivcvndetvr. ¶ Considered by Daniel, Wackernagel, and Koch, to be fourteenth century work. With a German translation beginning *Alle werlet freuet sich*, its first known appearance is in a Breslau MS., 1, 8, f. 113, of the latter part of the fifteenth century. See Daniel, I, p. 329, and IV, p. 260. Wackernagel, I, No. 358, p. 215, reprints Christ. Adolf's version (1542) and that of J. Spangenberg (1544). Chevalier, II, p. 264, mentions several other books where it may be found. ¶ *Omnis mundus iucundetur* re-appears in the vernacular as *Seydt frölich und jubilieret*, and *Alle Welt springe und lobsinge*; see Kehrein, 'Katholische Kirchenlieder' (1859), I, Nos. 116 and 117. ¶ For the earliest forms of the Melody see Zahn, V, No. 8581, *a* and *b*; and for

later

later variations, in triple and common time, see Meister, I, No. 29 (Bäumker, I, No. 49). ⁋ For settings in four-part harmony, see Mich. Prætorius, 'Mus. Sion.' (1607), Nos. xciii and xciv. See also M. Prætorius' *Polyhymnia Panegyrica* (Wolfenbüttel, 1618-1619), No. xv, where it is arranged for many voices and stringed instruments. M. Prætorius' No. xciv is evidently the descant to an older setting of the PIÆ CANTIONES melody, treated as a fresh air. See 'The Cowley Carol Book' (1908), No. 28 (i and ii), in which collection, as well as in 'Carols for Christmas-tide' (1853), No. II, will be found harmonies of this fourteenth or fifteenth century melody, set to Dr. Neale's carol beginning *Earthly friends will change and falter*. ⁋ Probably, at the first, in the Mixo-Lydian mode, but later on treated as a Lydian or Ionian melody. PIÆ CANTIONES has apparently adopted Cyriac Spangenberg's form of the tune (1568), but with a few trifling variations.

IX. DIES EST LÆTICIÆ. ⁋ *Ein gar alt freudenreich christlich Lied auff Weihnachten*, Leisentrit (1544); *Canticum veteris ecclesiæ* (Lossius); *Hymnus natalitius, vetus et vulgaris* (Paar); *vetus et insignis* (D. G. Corner). Probably of the twelfth century. Commonly ascribed to Benno, Bishop of Meissen (†1107); but by Koch supposed to be the work of Adam of St. Victor (†1177). According to another authority, the Latin text is of the fourteenth century. Dreves, in his *Cantiones Bohemicæ* ('Anal. Hymnica,' I, p. 42) finds *Dies est leticie* (i) in a Hohenfurth MS. of A.D. 1410; (ii) in a 'Kantional von Jistebnicz,' *c.* 1420; (iii) in a 'Graduale von Jistebnicz,' early fifteenth century; (iv) in another MS. of the beginning of the sixteenth century, all of them at Prag. For the text, Dreves refers his readers: (i) to Mone, I, No. 47, p. 62, where it is printed, in nine stanzas, from the Trier Hymner (No. 724, at München, of the fifteenth century); and from two other books posterior to PIÆ CANTIONES, which may therefore be dismissed; (ii) to Wackernagel, I, No. 332, pp. 206-7, this being a reprint of Adolf (1542); of Joh. Spangenberg (1544); Lossius (1553-1579); Joh. Leisentrit (1567) and the 'Tegernsee Book' (1577). See also Daniel, I, p. 330, and IV, p. 254. ⁋ *Dies est leticie* generally consists of eight or nine stanzas, though Lossius (1553) prints only

1, 2, 5 and 4. Like the Hohenfurth MS., Piæ Cantiones omits a verse after *Mundus dum describitur.* It runs as follows: 'Chriſtum natum dominum | omnes imploremus | matremque cum filio | pariter laudemus | : eſt ſatis mirabilis | et multum laudabilis | verè puer iſte|: Ergo ſolus dominus | ſolus et altiſſimus | es tu, Ieſu Chriſte.' Unlike the Hohenfurth MS., Piæ Cantiones omits the following verſe: 'Mater, tuum filium | iugiter implora | vt nobis remedium | ſit in mortis hora. | Qui luctamur ſtadio | demonis incendio | camino penali, | ſed accepto brauio | letemur cum filio | veſte nuptiali.' Joh. Spangenberg (1544) gives an additional verſe for Epiphany—for *Dies eſt leticie* was ſung "auff den heiligen Chriſtag, newe jahrs tag, und auch uff das Feſt Epiphanie"— 'Ut ſtellam conſpiciunt | viri ſapientes | ab oriente veniunt | ſecum afferentes | precioſa munera | chriſto valdè congrua | aurum, thus & myrrham | aurum regi inclyto | thus deo altiſſimo | myrrham in ſepulturam.' ¶ The arrangement of the ſtanzas varies conſiderably: but, on the whole, Piæ Cantiones clearly follows the order of the Bohemian MSS. and Leiſentrit. As might be expected in a carol ſo widely circulated, there are many *variæ lectiones.* In St. i, Piæ Cant. inſerts the prepoſition 'de' before 'ventre'; it prefers the reading '*totus* delectabilis' rather than 'vultu delectabilis.' In St. ii, it reads 'ſtupeſcit natura *quem*,' where other books read '*quòd*,' and it chooſes 'lac pudicitiæ,' a better reading than 'lac pueritiæ.' In St. iv, the Trier MS. reads 'dum fulgur deſcendit' inſtead of 'ac fulgur accendit.' In St. vi, the old MSS. read 'Sic illæſa creditur | Virgo poſt & ante: | Felix eſt puerpera | cuius clauſa viſcera | deum portauerunt.' According to Mone, St. vii ran as follows: 'Orbis dum deſcribitur | virgo prægnans ibat | Bethlehem, quò naſcitur | puer qui nos ſcribat | in illorum curiam | qui canebant gloriam | ſummæ deitatis | et in terræ finibus | pax ſit in hominibus | bonæ voluntatis.' For notes and other leſs important variants, ſee Daniel, Meiſter, Wackernagel, Mone, and Julian. Piæ Cantiones text is reprinted in Klemming, II, p. 19. ¶ In his 'Kirchen und religioſe Lieder,' No. xiv, p. 221, Kehrein prints *Ein Kindelein ſo löbelich* from a MS. of the twelfth century. This has been continuouſly aſſociated with the melody of *Dies eſt leticie*, but is independent of the Latin words. ¶ In later German hymnbooks *Dies eſt leticie* appears in

216   the

the vernacular, as *Der tag der iſt ſo freudenreich*. In 'Then Swenſka Pſalmeboken' (1572) it appears in Swediſh as *Een iungfru födde itt barn j dagh*. To this melody was ſung *Når Adam i Paradijs* and *Nu må werlder frögda ſich*. See Rhezelius (1619), pp. 19 and 26. In Holland it became *Tis een dach van vrolichkeit*. ❡ The earlieſt known form of the Tune is

Hohenfurther Hs. 1410.

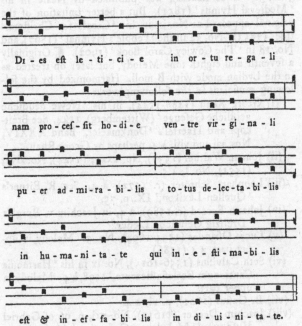

Di - es eſt le - ti - ci - e   in or - tu re - ga - li

nam pro - ceſ - ſit ho - di - e   ven - tre vir - gi - na - li

pu - er ad - mi - ra - bi - lis   to - tus de - lec - ta - bi - lis

in hu - ma - ni - ta - te   qui in - e - ſti - ma - bi - lis

eſt & in - ef - fa - bi - lis   in di - ui - ni - ta - te.

to be found in the aforeſaid Hohenfurth MS. at Prag, A.D. 1410. It is given by Dreves in his 'Cantiones Bohemicæ' ('Anal. Hymnica,' vol. I), No. xiii, p. 194. ❡ For the ſake of this deſervedly popular Melody many original poems have been written. For inſtance, Joh. Mauburn (†1503) compoſed his 'Eia mea anima,' the fourth verſe of which is 'Heu! quid iaces ſtabulo,' *ad praeſepij viſitationem, canendum ſub nota:* Dies eſt leticie.' See Daniel, I, No. ccccxxxi,

217   P. 335

p. 335; R. C. Trench's 'Sacred Latin Poetry' (1864),
p. 114; and 'Anal. Hymnica,' XLVIII, No. 494. To varying
forms of this Tune (which are given in Meifter, I, No. xxi,
pp. 168-174, and in Zahn, IV, Nos. 7869-7872) were fung
the following Chriftmas Carols: *Als Jefus geboren war, Als
Adam in Paradies*, and *Weil Maria fchwanger gieng*. ❡ A tranflation of *Dies eft leticie*, beginning *Royal day that chafeft
gloom* (in three ftanzas), was publifhed by Neale in his
'Medieval Hymns' (1851). But a better imitation of the
original appeared as No. ix in his 'Carols for Chriftmas-
tide' (1853); No. 34 in the 'People's Hymnal' (1867), and
No. 18 in 'The Cowley Carol Book' (1902). ❡ Originally
a feventh and eighth tone Melody, but later on treated as
in the Lydian mode with B moll. Harmonized by the following muficians in the following works:

  (i) Georg Rhau (1488-1544), in his 'Newe deudfche
      geiftliche Gefenge' (Wittemberg), 1544. See Breit-
      kopf and Haertel's 'Denkmaeler,' Band XXXIV,
      Nos. vii and viii, à 4, perhaps by Georg Rhau.

  (ii) Johann Walther (1537), No. xxxv; (1544), No. xlvi;
      (1551), No. l, à 5.

  (iii) Leonhart Schröter (*c.* 1572), à 4. See R. Eitner's
      'Quellen-Lexikon,' IX, p. 75.

  (iv) Johann Eccard (*c.* 1589), à 4, in Joachim v. Burgk's
      'Dreifzig Geiftliche Lieder.'

  (v) Lucas Ofiander (1534-1604), No. 3. Melody in up-
      per part, à 4 (1586).

  (vi) Seth Calvifius (1556-1615), No. ix in his 'Harmonia
      Cantionum Ecclefiafticarum,' 1598, à 4. Melody in
      upper part.

  (vii) B. Gefius (1601), p. xi, à 4.

  (viii) Joachim Decker (†1611), No. xxi, p. 96 of Gabriel
      Hufduvius' 'Melodeyen Gefangbuch' (1604), à 4.

  (ix) Gothardus Erythræus, 'Pfalmen und Geiftliche Lie-
      der' (1608), No. xxiii.

  (x) Michael Prætorius, Helmftadt (1607), Part III,
      No. v, for two quires of four voices; 'Mufæ
      Sioniæ,' V (1607), No. lxxv (à 4); No. lxxvi
      (à 4); No. lxxvii (à 3); No. lxxviii (à 4); No.
      lxxix (à 5); 'Mufæ Sioniæ,' VI (1609), No. xvi
      (à 4); No. xxx (à 4); No. lv (à 4).

Hieronymus

(xi) Hieronymus Prætorius, 'Cantiones Variæ' (Hamburg, 1618 and 1622), No. xxix, folio G, à 8.

(xii) Andreas Hammerſchmidt (1611-1675).

(xiii) Joh. Dilliger (1593-1647); 'Muſica Votiva' (1622), (cantus à 2, concert à 2, ad organon à 2).

(xiv) J. H. Schein's 'Cantional' (1645), Nos. x and xxvi.

(xv) Joh. Crüger (1649), in his 'Geiſtl. Kirchen-Melodien,' No. xl; in his 'Praxis Pietatis Melica' (1657), No. 90 (melody and figured baſs); in his 'Geiſtl. Lieder und Pſalmen,' No. xiv, arranged for four voices and three inſtruments; in his 'Prax. Piet. Mel.' (1690), No. 351, a ſetting by Jacob Hintze (1622-1702).

(xvi) 'Sirenes Symphoniacæ' (1678), à 4. See Meiſter, I, App. II, No. 26.

(xvii) Dietrich Buxtehude (1637-1707) in his 'Orgel Compoſitionen' (Breitkopf and Haertel, Band II, Pt. II, No. 3).

(xviii) Joh. Pachelbel (1653-1706); Breitkopf, Denkmaeler, Bd. iv, No. 18.

(xix) Joh. Seb. Bach (1685-1750), as No. 158 in '371 Vierſtimmige Choral-geſänge'; alſo in his 'Choral-preludes for the Organ' (Breitkopf, Band VII, No. 10; Band VIII, No. 86); 'Bach Geſellſchaft,' No. 41.

(xx) Friedrich Layriz, in his 'Kern des deutſchen Kirchengeſangs' (1855), No. 26, à 4.

(xxi) 'Kath. Geſangbuch' (St. Gallen), 1863, No. 14.

(xxii) Neale and Helmore's 'Carols for Chriſtmas-tide' (1853), No. ix.

(xxiii) 'Haus-Choralbuch' (Güterſloh), 1887, No. 14.

(xxiv) 'Cowley Carol Book' (1902), No. 18, and 'Songs of Syon' (1910), No. 417 (Prætorius ſetting, 1609, 'Mus. Sion.,' No. lv).

❡ Beſides the above named ſources, ſome form or other of the melody of *Dies eſt leticie* is to be found harmonized in nearly every reſpectable Catholick or Lutheran tune book, too many to be enumerated, down from the ſixteenth to the twentieth century. ❡ Neale, in his Medieval Hymns, (1851), p. 132, deſcribes *Dies eſt leticie* as ' a German Carol; at leaſt it does not ſeem to have been uſed in the offices of

the

the Church. It is perhaps scarcely worth mentioning that Luther believed it inspired.' ❡ For further information, see Julian, pp. 294 and 295.

X. CONGAVDEAT TVRBA FIDELIVM. ❡ A Christmas Trope on *Benedicamus Domino.* Two forms of this interesting carol, earlier than P. C. text, are extant. (A) That printed by E. du Méril, II, p. 47, and thence reproduced by Neale in his 'Hymni ecclesiæ' (1851), p. 228, and by Daniel (1855), IV, p. 147. This occurs in an eleventh century MS., No. 1139, in the Bibl. Reg., Paris, f. 61, verso; (B) That given by Amédée Gastoué in the 'Revue du Chant Grégorien,' Sept., 1902, p. 24. The latter is taken from an Antiphonale Missarum of the twelfth century (notation Aquitaine), once in use at the Church of St. Peter at Apt (Apta Julia), a city in the department of Vaucluse, about thirty miles E. of Avignon. Gastoué describes this particular carol as 'a delightful Cantilene, ancestor, probably, or at least one of the most ancient representatives of popular Noëls.' Thanks to Mr. E. G. P. Wyatt, we are here able to print the Apt version of the words, and tune of this venerable Carol. See p. 221.

(A) 1 Congaudeat turba fidelium
        natus est rex saluator omnium   in betleem.
     2 Laudem celi nunciat angelus,
        et in terris pacem hominibus   in betleem.
     3 Loquebantur pastores inuicem,
        transeamus ad nouum hominem   in betleem.
     4 In presepe et bos et asinus
        Cognouerunt quod esset dominus   in betleem.
     5 Tunc herodes querit perimere
        quem deberet orandum querere   in betleem.
     6 In egyptum maria filium
        transfert, timens regis imperium   in betleem.
     7 Ex humana virgine nascitur
        quo nascente gaudens efficitur   Iherusalem.
     8 Benedicat plebs ergo virginem
        venter cuius celorum pertulit   artificem.
     9 Rege nato sydus exoritur
        quo previo regum coniungitur societas.   [MS. peruio]
    10 Par est inter parem intentio   [l. pares?]
        pari querunt regem consilio   quo liceat.   [l. quo iaceat?]
    11 * Regnunt, intrant, regem reperiunt,   * [l. adsunt?]
        cui aurum, thus, myrrham offerunt   et gracias.

(B) APT ANTIPHONALE (xij cent.)

En gau - de - at tur - ba fi - de - li - um, ma - ter

vir - go pe - pe - rit fi - li - um in beth - le - em.

(B) 1 En gaudeat turba fidelium
          mater virgo peperit filium in betleem.
    2 [Same as A].
    3 [Same as A and Piæ Cant.].
    4 Cui magi, notato sydere,
          donant eum mystico munere in betleem.
    5 Quem donantes munere mystico
          benedicunt celorum domino in betleem.
    6 [Same as A's fourth St.].
    7 [Same as A's sixth St.].
    8 Benedicta sint matris vbera
          lactantia regem . . . in betleem.
    9 Carnem nostram quam deo socias
          tibi, virgo, redd[amus gracias] in betleem.

❡ Comparison of the above with the Piæ Cantiones version shows that stanzas 2, 5, 6, and 7 are peculiar to Petri's book. ❡ The last stanza of P. C. requires notice:

          Collyridas simul cum nectare
          Benedicat Christus Rex gloriæ in Bethlehem.

Collyrida was apparently a kind of Simnel cake, something like the French *Pain béni*. It was composed of coarse meal, and of sweet olive oil with honey; in shape, square or triangular. *Collyridam panis quoddam genus esse memento* (Alexander Poeta). The two following passages from Du Cange's 'Glossarium' (Paris, 1733), II, p. 770, prove that it was the custom at Christmas and Pentecost to distribute largesses in the forms of these bakemeats or *Collyridæ*. It was, perhaps, a survival of the early Christian Agapæ. 'Item debet dare dictus dominus Abbas dicto conuentui in singulis festivitatibus . . . Pentecostes . . . triginta libras

221   panis

panis frumenti . . . necnon *nectar & colleridas* sufficienter
& semel duntaxat quolibet anno, & non in quolibet
dictorum festorum.' (Transactio inter Abbatem et Mona-
chos Crassenses, anno 1351); and again, 'Item tenetur dare
Pitantiarius in die Natalis Domini . . . tres *coleridas* siue
mensas pro quacunque pitantia.' (In statutis S. Victoris,
anno 1531). ¶ It is interesting to compare the earlier free-
rhythm form of the music-note (in the Dorian mode) as
given by the Apt Antiphonale of the twelfth century with
the later sixteenth century metrical version as it stands in
PIÆ CANTIONES.

¶ In Rhezelius (1619), p. 47, the PIÆ CANTIONES tune is
accurately reproduced, set to the Swedish words *Sigh glädia
må alt menniskligh kön.* ¶ Neale has caught the spirit of this
venerable old carol in his *From Church to Church the bells'
glad tidings run* ('Carols for Christmas-tide,' 1853, No. VII).
But unfortunately the music there was misinterpreted. For
two correct settings, see 'The Cowley Carol Book' (1902),
No. 7.

XI. PVER NOBIS NASCITVR. ¶ At Christmas instead of
Benedicamus Domino. Mone, I, No. 48, p. 64, reprints this
carol from a fifteenth-century MS., No. 724 in the Stadt-
bibliothek at Trier [T]. Wackernagel, I, Nos. 327-331,
gives five versions: (i) from the Trier library; (ii) from a
MS. at München, Cod. Lat. 5023, fifteenth century [M];
(iii) from Christ. Adolf's printed book of 1542 [A]; (iv) from
J. Spangenberg of 1544 [S]; (v) from J. Leisentrit, 1567 [L];
besides later forms found in the Speier, Mainz, and Paderborn song-books. Dreves ('Analecta Hymnica,' I, p. 43)
mentions the fact that *Puer nobis nascitur* occurs (i) in the
Hohenfurth MS. of 1410 [H]; and (ii) in the Wittingau
MS. of 1459 [W]. Again the great number of variations
testifies to the wide use of this favourite *Cantio.* The order
of the stanzas is irregular, and the number of verses ranges
from four to seven. ¶ Comparing PIÆ CANTIONES [P. C.]
with the older versions:

In St. I, P. C. reads *panditur*; but all the other authorities
   have *pascitur,* except A, which prefers *patitur.*
St. II. P. C. reads *positum,* the rest *ponitur*; Leisentrit and
   the later books omit *sub* before *fæno asinorum.*

For

St. III. For *Hunc* in P. C. and L, T, M, W, A, and S read *Hinc*; M has *Quem*. P. C., S, H, and W read *Magno cum tremore*, but M and T have *dolore*; L, *timore*; A, *liuore*. Unlike the rest, P. C. reads *In infantes irruit*, but T has *Et pueros occidit infantes cum liuore*; M, *Infantes et pueros occidit cum cruore*; H, *Infantesque puerulos*; A and S have *Occidit cum dolore*; and L, *necat præ dolore*.

St. IV. W and A read *Qui natus de virgine*; T, M, and S, *Qui natus est ex maria*; L has *Puer natus in Bethlehem*; W has *perduc nos cum gracia*; T, *ducat nos cum gracia*; M, *producat nos ad gaudia* | *cum gracia superna*; A and S, *perducat nos*.

St. V. H reads *Alpha, I & E & O* (thrice); M has *A & I & E & O*; T reads *O & A et A & O*; A has *Cantemus in choro*; S, *Canimus in choro*; T, M, and S, *Cum cantibus in choro* | *cum canticis et organo*; and A, *in chordis et organo*.

❡ These variants have not been compared with the MSS. above quoted, but are here printed on the authority of Mone, Wackernagel, and Dreves, assuming their details to be correct. ❡ In Rhezelius (1619), p. 33, the P. C. form of the tune is repeated with the Swedish words *Itt Barn år osz nu hår födt*. ❡ The melody is in the Lydian mode with B moll, practically the modern major scale. Various forms of the Tune are to be seen in Zahn, No. 1569 *a* and *b*, and in Meister, I (No. 38). ❡ For harmonies see (i) Michael Prætorius, 'Mus. Sion.,' VI (1609), No. xliv, à 4; (ii) 'Sirenes Symphoniacæ,' Cöln (1678), as given by Meister, I, App. ii, No. 33; (iii) 'The Cowley Carol Book' (1902), No. 25, where it is set to English words, a translation of PIÆ CANTIONES. ❡ *Geborn ist Gottes Sönelein* (iambic 8.8.8.8), (see M. Prætorius, 'Mus. Sion.,' 1609, and 'The Cowley Carol Book,' No. 21), is a corrupt following of the older melody. *Puer nobis nascitur* is best known in Germany as *Uns ist geborn ein Kindelein*.

XII. PVER NATVS IN BETHLEHEM. ❡ A Christmas-tide *Benedicamus Domino*, of Bohemian origin. Like *In dulci iubilo*, long ascribed, but erroneously so, to Peter Faulfisch of Dresden, *c.* 1412. ❡ Three distichs of this carol, viz., those beginning *Puer natus in bethleem, Assumpsit carnem hominis*,

and

and *Cognouit bos et afinus* are contained in an Antiphoner MS., from Bobbio, Cod. Taurinen, F 1 4, of the end of the thirteenth century ('Anal. Hymnica,' XX, No. 111, p. 99). Dreves had already difcovered *Puer natus in bethleem* in five different MSS., all of them at Prag (fee 'Anal. Hymnica,' I, No. 178, p. 163), the firft of thefe being a *Proceffionale* once belonging to the Benedictine Nuns of the Convent of St. George on the Hradfchin. This is known as the Prager Hfch., XIII, H. 3. C., *circa* 1320. The fecond of thefe five MSS. is the Huffite 'Kantional von Jiftebnicz,' *circa* 1420. *Puer natus in bethleem* is alfo found in a MS. of the fourteenth century at München (Wackernagel, I, No. 309); and it occurs as a profe in the printed Hereford Breviary of 1505 (fee 'Henry Bradfhaw Society,' Vol. XXVI, 1903, p. 19, Part I, *In die Epyphanie in Laudibus*). In the Prag MSS. it confifts of thefe nine or ten couplets: (1) Puer natus in bethleem; (2) Affumpfit carnem hominis; (3) Per Gabrielem nuncium; (4) Tanquam fponfus de thalamo; (5) Ponitur in prefepio; (6) Cognouit bos et afinus; (7) Reges de Saba veniunt; (8) Intrantes domum inuicem; (9) Trino uni fempiterno | benedicamus domino; (10) Sit benedicta trinitas | deo dicamus gracias; *or* Ei femper angelicas | deo dicamus gracias. ❡ 'This hymn, of a very beautiful fimplicity, and abforbing eafily and naturally fo much theology in its poetry, and in many ways containing fo much in a brief compafs' (R. C. Trench, 'Sacred Latin Poetry,' 1849, p. 93) may be feen in various forms in Wackernagel, I, Nos. 309-316; alfo in Daniel, I, No. 480, p. 334. For further information fee Julian, p. 940. ❡ Piæ Cantiones includes moft of the later additional couplets given in Wackernagel. Its chief variations from older readings may be attributed to the influence of Hermann Bonn, the Lutheran, who, as Loffius informs us in his 'Pfalmodia' (1561), p. 27*b*, 'corrected' this *Benedicamus*. In St. II, P. C. reads *Affumfit carnem hominis | verbum Patris altiffimi*. This mars the rime: the Prag MSS. read *Affumpfit carnem filius | dei patris altiffimus*; the Hereford Brev. has *Affumpfit carnem filij | dei patris altiffimi*. In St. III the older books read *Per Gabrielem nuncium*. In St. VII, Hereford reads *progrediens ex vtero*. In St. VIII, P. C. reads *Hic iacet in præfepio*, but the Prag MSS. prefer *Ponitur in prefepio*, or *Imponitur*

prefepio;

prefepio; while Hereford has *Se ponit in prefepio | regnabit fine termino*. In St. XI, P. C. has altered *Reges de Saba veniunt* (Hereford *venient* and *offerent*) into *Magi de longè veniunt*; and in St. XII, *Nouum falutant principem*, as in the Prag MSS., and *falutant nouum hominem* has been changed into *natum falutant hominem*. In P. C. the laft two verfes differ from the older authorities. Hereford confifts in all of nine ftanzas, the laft of which is *Trino deo fempiterno | benedicamus domino*. Klemming, II, p. 17, reprints the PIÆ CANTIONES verfion. Before the penultimate Strophè the Mainz Hymner (1631) inferts 'Gloria tibi domine | qui natus es de virgine.'

❡ On Stanza IX (*Cognouit bos et afinus*) the learned H. A. Daniel has a valuable note. As his 'Thefaurus Hymnologicus' is now out of print and rare, here is the paffage. 'Notum eft fere in omnibus imaginibus, quæ Nativitatem domini repræfentant, bouis afinique figuras exhiberi nec quidquam poetis pictoribufque certius eft, quam hæc animalia in illo diuerforio adfuiffe. . . . *In einem crippffli lit ein kind | do ftot ein efel und ein rind. . . . Do ftund ein efel und ein rind | und dientend im getrate.* Orta eft hæc narratio ex loco Habacuci, c. III, 2. LXX, ἐν μέσῳ δύο ζώων γνωσθήσῃ, vetufta verfione latina: *in medio duorum animalium innotefceris*. Bouem vero et afinum finxerunt fibi ex loco Is. I, 3. 'Cognouit bos poffefforem fuum et afinus præfepe domini fui.' Hanc prophetiam nocte Natiuitatis domini impletam effe credebant. Pelb. Pomoer. Serm. Hym. XVI: *bruta animalia teftata funt miraculo deitatem Chrifti, quia cum mater fancta puerum natum Chriftum in præfepio locaffet bos et afinus ad præfepium illud ligati miraculofe Deum cognofcentes flexis genibus ipfum adorauerunt et à fæno illo abftinuerunt*. Sed nihil hi vetufti ad Zach. Wernerum hæc de animalibus narrantem: . . . *Seine göttliche Mutter wickelte ihn in Windeln und legte ihn in eine Krippe, zwifchen zwei unfchuldigen Thieren, einem Ochfen und einem Efel, welche fo glücklich waren den Herrn zu fehen. Endlich von des Oechfeleins und Efeleins Hauch erwärmt fchlug das Kindelein die Augen auf und weinte.* Daniel, I, No. cccclxxx, p. 335.

❡ This Carol occurs in a fourteenth-fifteenth century paper MS. in the Brit. Mus. [Add. MS. 5666]. The latter is described by Mr. A. Hughes-Hughes as 'A small collection of Carols, etc., probably written for two or three voices, though in one or two cases only one part is given. Said by T. Martin, of Palgrave, to be in the hand of John Brackley, friar minor of Norwich, tutor to William Paston, Justice of the Common Pleas [1378-1444]. Brackley was still living in 1461. At the end are some memoranda by John Whyte, *tempp.* Richard II and Henry IV.' On f. 8*b* is written *Puer natus in betlehem*. The Text consists of the following seven distichs, beginning respectively: (i) Puer natus; (ii) Assumpsit carnem; (iii) Per Gabrielem; (iv) Sicut sponsus; (v) Cognouit bos; (vi) Intrantes domum; and (vii) Benedicamus dño. The Tune (quite different from that in Piæ Cantiones) is apparently arranged for two voices, but it is unworthy of reproduction.

❡ Wackernagel, II, Nos. 904-907, gives several German translations of this 'canticum vulgare,' this 'alt geistlich lied.' They date from the fifteenth century and begin thus *Ein Kint geparn czu bethlehem*, sung at Christmas in the vernacular alternately with the Latin. *Die künig von Saba kamen dar* was repeated at the Epiphany.

❡ *Puer natus in Bethlehem* appears in the 'Svenska Psalmeboken' of 1572 as *Itt Barn àr födt j Bethlehem;* and as *Itt lijtet Barn àr osz födt nu* in Rhezelius (1619), p. 30. For English translations see Julian, p. 940 (ii). ❡ For various forms of the Piæ Cantiones melody, or rather melodies, to which *Puer natus in Bethlehem* was sung, see Meister, I, Nos. 30-31, pp. 193-198; Bäumker, I, Nos. 51 and 52; and Zahn, I, No. 192 *a* and *b*, p. 53. The tune assigned by P. C. to the tenor voice (in the Dorian mode) is undoubtedly the older of the two. That was the Plainsong, to which the second tune (entrusted by Piæ Cantiones to the Bass) in the Hypo-Dorian mode, was nevertheless in reality the Descant. By degrees the latter supplanted the old Plainsong and came to be treated as a distinct air in itself. In Lucas Lossius' 'Psalmodia' (1561 and 1569) the two melodies occur as tenor and descant: but in his 1579 edition there occurs a setting for four voices, the descant preserving its form, but the tenor already being altered for the worse. In 'The Cowley Carol Book' (1902), No. 1, the two Piæ Cantiones tunes have been

226   retained

retained in their integrity, with the addition of two other parts (alto and bafs).

❡ *Puer natus in Bethlehem* has been repeatedly harmonized and arranged for vocal and inftrumental purpofes, and may be found in the following works and elfewhere:

(i) 'Obfequiale Eccles. Ratifbon.' (1570).

(ii) J. Leifentrit's 'Geiftliche Lieder' (1573).

(iii) Nicolas Selneccer, 'Chriftliche Pfalmen, etc.' (1587), p. 588.

(iv) Lucas Ofiander, 'Fünfftzig Geiftliche Lieder und Pfalmen' (1586), No. 7, à 4.

(v) Lucas Loffius' 'Pfalmodia,' *vide fupra*.

(vi) Seth Calvifius (1556-1615), 'Harmonia cant. ecclefiafticarum' (1598), No. iiii. Alfo in Barth. Gefius' 'Geiftl. Deutfche Lieder' (1601), p. 17, à 4; and p. 18, à 5.

(vii) Gabriel Hufduvius' 'Melodeyen G. B.' (Hamburg, 1604), No. lxxii, p. 294, harmonized by David Scheidemann.

(viii) Erhard Bodenfchatz (1570-1636), 'Harm. Angelica Cant. Ecclefiafticarum' (1608), for which fee Meifter, I, pp. 196-7.

(ix) Michael Prætorius (1572-1621), 'Mus. Sion.,' V (1607); (i) No. lxxxiv, à 4; (ii) No. lxxxv, à 5; (iii) No. lxxxvi, à 6. 'Mus. Sion.' (Jehnæ, 1607); (i) No. vi, for double quire; (ii) No. vii, à 8 (*In Regal vel clavicymbalo vel altero organo et una voce*). 'Mus. Sion.,' VI (1609); (i) No. xxxiv (Marck. Thür.); (ii) No. xxxv (Seeftedt); (iii) No. xxxvi (Schw. Fran.), à 4, each. 'Polyhymnia Panegyrica' (Wolffenbüttel, 1618-1619), No. xii, an elaborate fetting for *capella vocalis* and *capella fidicinaria*.

(x) Hieronymus Prætorius (1560-1629), 'Cantiones Variæ' (Hamburg, 1618), f. F. 3, No. xxvii, à 8.

(xi) Joh. Stobæus (1586-1646), quoted by Winterfeld, II, p. 134.

(xii) Martin Zeuner (1616); fee Winterfeld, II, p. 24.

(xiii) Joh. Hermann Schein (1586-1630), in his 'Cantional' (1627 and 1645); No. xi, p. 22. See Meifter, I, p. 196.

(xiv) Joh. Crüger (1598-1662), (i) in Tim. Kitzfchen's

227   'Geiftl.

'Geiſtl. Kirchen-Melodien' (1649), for four voices, violins and horns, No. 49.

(ii) In his 'Praxis Pietatis Melica' (1656), No. 110 (melody and baſs).

(xv) D. Buxtehude (c. 1637-1707); Organ works. See Breitkopf and Haertel, Band XIV (1903).

(xvi) Joh. Gottfried Walther (1684-1748), for Organ: Breitkopf, Bände XXVI-XXVII, No. 81, p. 200.

(xvii) Joh. Seb. Bach (1685-1750) (i) in his 'Orgel Muſik.' Breitkopf, Band VII, No. 39.

(ii) *Cantata am Feſte der heiligen drei Könige (Sie werden aus Saba alle kommen)* for four voices with Flauti and Oboe di Caccia accompaniment. (iii) 'Orgel-werke,' Band II, Orgelbüchlein, p. 6. See alſo Bach's '371 Vierſtimmige Choral-geſange,' No. 12; in 'The Cowley Carol Book' (1902), No. 1.

(xviii) F. Layriz' 'Kern des deutſchen Kirchengeſangs' (1854), No. 308.

❡ Another Melody for *Puer natus in Bethlehem*, older than thoſe in PIÆ CANTIONES, quite diſtinct from them and in a different mode, is to be found in 'Anal. Hymnica,' I (Beilagen, Nos. xvi and xvii, pp. 195-6). No. xvi is taken from the Prag MS., *circa* 1320; and No. xvii gives the ſame tune as it appears about 100 years later, viz., in the 'Kantional von Jiſtebnicz,' *circa* 1420. After another interval of a century and upwards, the ſame fine melody reappears ſlightly modified in J. Spangenberg's 'Geſang-buch' 1544, and in Lucas Loſſius. Spangenberg's verſion is ſet to Engliſh words *To us is born a little Child*, and is harmonized for uniſon ſinging in 'The Cowley Carol Book' (1902), No. 23. This melody alſo is of Bohemian parentage.

XIII. AD CANTVS LÆTICIÆ. ❡ Quoted by Dreves ('Anal. Hymnica,' XX, No. 9, p. 80) from four ſources: Trop. MS. Cod. Stuttgartien., thirteenth century (A); Cod. Engel-bergen., fourteenth century (B); Proceſs. MS. Schonen-bergenſe, 1533 (C); Cod. Berolinen. fifteenth century (D). Wackernagel (I, No. 390, p. 233) gives Chriſtian Adolf's verſion, 1542 (E). In St. I, A and B read *Ad cantum*; C, D, and E *Ad feſtum*. St. II. ABCDE read *quem*

228 *prædixit.*

prædixit. Before St. III BCDE insert the quatrain, 'Ivdea gens misera | corde, verbis propera, | potes esse libera | si credis'; but E reads *crede* for *corde,* and in the fourth line C and E have *si velis* instead of *si credis.* In the last stanza C, D, and E read Ergo nunc cum gaudio | nostra simul concio; B, Ergo nostra concio | psallens cum tripudio; A, Ergo nostra concio | summo cum tripudio. ❡ Piæ Cantiones text is reprinted by Klemming, II, p. 11. ❡ T. Norlind ('Svensk Musik-historia,' 1901, p. 18) refers to Ad cantvs lætitiæ as an early and interesting instance of Rondo-form music. In 'The Cowley Carol Book' (1902), No. 40, this *Cantio* is set to English words, as well as to the Latin. The *Prima Vox* starts there on the fourth beat of the first bar, and the *Altera Vox* on the first beat of the second bar. ❡ In the Hypo-Ionian Mode.

XIV. Gavdete, gavdete Christvs est natvs. ❡ Text reprinted by Klemming (1886), p. 28. ❡ The four-part setting, in close score, with the Plainsong probably in the Tenor, stands as given by Piæ Cantiones. ❡ Rhezelius, in his 'Någre Psalmer' (1619), prints a Swedish translation of this *Gaudete,* with instruction that it is to be sung to the tune of *Vitamq faciunt beatiorem,* i.e. 'Vitam quæ faciant beatiorem,' by Martial, Epp., Lib. X, No. 47, the same metre as Catullus' 'Viuamus, mea Lesbia, atque amemus,' No. v. in the metre technically known as the Hendecasyllabic Phalecian, consisting of a spondee, a dactyl, and three trochees. Rhezelius (*ibid.*) gives the option of another melody, that of *Tacker Herra nom som a ganska blijder,* whatever that may be. According to Zahn (Vol. I of his 'Die Melodien,' etc., pp. 7 and 8, No. 12) it was Joh. Spangenberg (in his 'Gramaticæ latinæ partes . . . in usum iuuentutis Northusianæ congestae, . . . 1546'), who first printed a four-part setting of *Vitam quæ faciunt beatiorem,* which setting is almost, note for note, identical with that of *Gaudete, gaudete, Christus est natus* in Piæ Cantiones. But it will be observed that *Ex Maria virgine, gaudete* is one syllable short, and fails to coincide with the metre of *iucundissime Martialis, hæc sunt.* Zahn further informs us that the above setting, to the words *Danket dem Herren, denn er ist so freundlich,* is to be found in Nigidius (1550); in Rihel (1569); in Sunderreiter (1581);

and

and elsewhere. He also mentions that the Tenor Melody
had already been twice harmonized in Ludwig Senfl's collection (1534); that, though the Descant lived on until
1648—being harmonized as a distinct melody by B. Gesius
(1601), and by M. Prætorius (1612), and others—yet in
the long run (contrary to the general rule and unlike the
fate, *e.g.*, of *Puer natus in Bethlehem*) the upper part failed
to get the upper hand of the Air in the Tenor, which
latter, true to its name, has held its own, and has been
fairly well known from 1546 down to the present day.
❡ This *Gaudete* is possibly a Refrain to the *Cantio* that
follows, *Tempus adest gratiæ:* but it will be noticed that,
unlike the rest of PIÆ CANTIONES, no tune for the latter is
provided. Was it an oversight on the editor's part, a
printer's error? Or was the quire expected, without rubric,
to sing this *Cantio* to the tune of *Tempus adest floridum*
(No. LII)? ❡ It is remarkable that the 3rd stanza, *Ezechielis
porta*, is found in one or other of three MSS. of the early
fifteenth and sixteenth centuries at Prag (Dreves, 'Cantiones
Bohemicæ,' I, No. 80, p. 107), with the Rundreim 'Gaudete,
gaudete | cum domino nascente | mundus renouatus est |
populo mirante.' | cf. PIÆ CANT., St. 11. According to some
authorities, it was sung to *Singuli catholice* (see Dreves, I, No.
129, p. 138), from the Prag MS., VI, B. 24, early sixteenth century. ❡ In the Dorian, or Hypo-Dorian Mode, transposed.

XV. CHRISTUS PRO NOBIS PASSVS. ❡ BENEDICAMVS, de
morte et resurrectione Christi, correctum per M. Herman:
Bonnum. See Christ. Adolf (1542), Joh. Walther (1543),
Luc. Loßius, 1553, 1561, 1569, and 1579; also Wack., I,
No. 476. In Rhezelius, p. 104, the P. C. form of the tune
is faithfully repeated, wedded to Swedish words, *Christus
leedh för osz dödhen swår.* ❡ Neale's *Sing alleluia, all ye
lands* is an imitation, rather than a translation, of the original.
See 'Carols for Easter-tide' (1854), No. xviii; and No. 57
in 'The Cowley Carol Book' (1902). ❡ In the last line
but one of the music, PIÆ CANTIONES, whether on purpose
or otherwise, has altered one note, and reads over the
words *et mortuus imperium*, g, c, d, e, D, c, b, a, instead of
g, c, d, e, E, c, b, a. Loßius' older version is set to *Veni,
veni, Emmanuel* in 'Songs of Syon' (1910), No. 8. It

230   appears

appears in Lobwaſſer (1579), as *Chriſtus das rechte Oſterlamm:* and is given in Zahn, No. 2580. In a ſlightly altered form it occurs in Michael Prætorius' 'Mus. Sion.' (1609), VI, No. cxli, ſet to the words *Jeſus Chriſtus wahr Gottes Sohn,* à 4; alſo, to the ſame words, in Gabriel Huſduvius' 'Melodeyen Geſangbuch' (Hamburg), 1604, harmonized by Joach. Decker (†1611), No. xlii, p. 206.

XVI. JESVS HVMANI GENERIS. ❡ Written by a man whoſe name was Johannes, as proved by the acroſtic. Reprinted by Klemming, II, p. 81, and thence incorporated in Dreves (XLV*b*, No. 173, p. 139). In the laſt verſe Dreves' reading *matris piæ hortamine,* inſtead of P. C.'s *patris pij hortamine,* an obvious alteration of older words, has been adopted. ❡ The melody is in the Dorian mode. It is to be found harmonized and ſet to Engliſh words (*Jeſus, to ſave mankind forlorn*) in 'The Cowley Carol Book' (1902), No. 54.

XVII. CEDIT HYEMS EMINVS. ❡ In reſurrectione domini ſuper 'Gloria in excelſis' Cantio; (Hohenfurth MS., A.D. 1410). Reprinted in Klemming, II, p. 108. ❡ The firſt ſtanza of P. C. agrees with the Hohenfurth MS., and with two other MSS. at Prag of the early part of the fifteenth and ſixteenth centuries. Dreves ('Cantiones Bohemicæ,' I, No. 62, p. 98); but in l. 4 Hohenfurth reads *terra* for *vallis.* P. C.'s firſt ſtanza agrees alſo with Leiſentrit (1567), as given by Wackernagel, I, No. 410, p. 242, and by Daniel, I, No. ccccxci, p. 342; but the remaining four ſtanzas are entirely different from the Bohemian texts. The laſt four lines of the third verſe of Adam of St. Victor's *Mundi renouatio* are very like P. C.; Celum fit ſerenius | et mare tranquillius | ſpirat aura leuius | : vallis noſtra floruit | reuireſcunt arida | recaleſcunt frigida | poſt quæ ver intepuit; ſee 'Clichtovei Elucidatorium,' p. 164, and Daniel, II, No. lxxxiv, p. 68.

❡ The Tenor, which eventually ſuperſeded the Canto Fermo (in the Baſs), is here given, but at No. LIX of the preſent work the Tenor, with Deſcant and Baſs, is given in full. ❡ For various forms of the original melody (in the Baſs) and for ſettings with the Tenor in the upper-

moſt

most part, see Zahn, No. 4974. The Bass melody appears in Michael Weisse [*geburtig von d' Neisse*], in his 'Ein new Gesengbuchlen,' 1531, set to the German words *Weltlich Ehr und zeitlich Gut* (f. k. ix *verso*).

¶ *Cedit hyems eminus* has been harmonized:

   (i) by Triller (1555), à 2;

   (ii) by B. Gesius (1601), p. 103, à 4;

   (iii) by M. Prætorius ('Mus. Sion.,' VII, 1609), Nos. 169-172; cf. Winterfeld, I, p. 282;

   (iv) by Joh. Crüger (1649) in his 'Geistliche Kirchen-Melodien,' No. 115, for voices and instruments;

   (v) by Joh. Crüger in his 'Praxis Pietatis Melica' (1656), with a Bass part added to the old Tenor melody;

   (vi) by Joh. Seb. Bach, No. 211, in his '371 Vierstim-mige Choräle'; and 'Bach Gesellschaft' (1889), No. 173.

   (vii) by B. Luard Selby in 'The Cowley Carol Book' (1902), No. 53, set to an English translation of the PIÆ CANTIONES words, beginning *Winter-tide hath past away.*

XVIII. IVCVNDARE IVGITER. ¶ The text reprinted by Klemming, II, p. 83. ¶ The Tune in the Dorian mode. Tenor only here given. But for Tenor, with Descant and Bass, as printed in PIÆ CANTIONES, see No. LX of this work. For a 4 pt. harmony, with the Canto Fermo (as it is supposed) in the uppermost part, set to English words, see 'Songs of Syon' (1910), No. 413.

XIX. TRIFORMIS RELVCENTIA. ¶ THOMAS *FECIT*. Peculiar to PIÆ CANTIONES. Thence copied by Klemming, II, p. 8, and so from Klemming into 'Anal. Hymnica,' XLV*b*, No. 177, p. 143. In stanza II, l. 1, PIÆ CANTIONES had trans-posed the words *hæc* and *lux*, thereby spoiling the Acrostic. Dreves' correction is right. In stanza III, l. 3, instead of leaving out any word, as Dreves proposes, scan the line thus, *ăb ŭtrŏquĕ mānăt Spiritus*. ¶ The melody is in the Lydian mode with B moll. ¶ In the original here, as in many other cases, the words are not accurately ranged beneath the Music-note. Consequently the slurring of certain passages has been difficult and occasionally conjectural.

XX. DIVINVM MYSTERIVM. ¶ A Trope to the *Sanctus*; also used for a Sequence ['Anal. Hymnica,' IX, No. 46]. Printed (*a*) by Mone, I, No. 240, p. 305, from an Hymner at München, Clm, 17,212, xii Jahrh. [M]; (*b*) by Dreves ['Anal. Hymnica,' IX, No. 46, p. 38], from Missale MS. Novesiense, sec. xv, Cod. Parisiens. 12,063 [N][1]; (*c*) by Dreves, XLVII, No. 319, p. 333, *q.v.* Dreves finds *Diuinum mysterium* in no fewer than twenty different MSS., Italian, German, Gallican, and Bohemian, ranging from the tenth to the sixteenth century. In the face of a certain St. Gallen MS. of the tenth century, the ascription of this Trope to St. Thomas Aquinas cannot be maintained. ¶ PIæ CANTIONES version, reproduced by Klemming (vol. II, p. 67), differs from the München MS. [M] and the 'Missale Novesiense' [N] chiefly in the following respects: by reading in St. I, *modo* instead of *semper*; *execratur* for *excæcatur*; *firma spe credentium* | *fides roboratur* instead of *firma spes credentium* | *fide roboratur*.

PIæ CANTIONES has inverted the order of the next four verses. *Fides est summoperè* comes before *Panis primo cernitur*, and *Et vinum similiter*. P. C.'s Doxology, *Pater, Nate, Spiritus* is not found in the old MSS.

In St. II, M reads thus: Panis prius cernitur | et tunc consecratur | caro tunc efficitur | panis sic mutatur | quomodo conuertitur? | deus operatur | . The same stanza appears in N, thus: Panis prius cernitur | sed dum consecratur | Corpus tunc efficitur | Christi, sic mutatur | quomodo conuertitur | deus operatur | .

In St. III, M has De vino similiter | si sit benedictum | (cum sit benedictum [N]) Ex tunc est veraciter | Christi sanguis dictum | credamus communiter, etc. A St. Gallen MS. of the fourteenth century has *tunc erit veraciter*.

In St. IV, an Engelberg MS. reads *panem suum* for *panem sanctum*. M and N read *Sumite* for *Sumere*; but PIæ CANTIONES *Sumere*, as a true rime with *summopere* and *edere*, is much to be preferred.

In St. V, N reads *tale Sacramentum* and *omnibus negantibus*,

[1] G. M. Dreves published *Divinum mysterium* in 1890 among *Sequentiæ Ineditæ*, but it is due to the memory of Francis J. Mone to record the fact that *Divinum mysterium* had already been edited by him and printed in his 'Hymni Latini Medij Ævi,' so far back as the year 1853.

and

and in the laſt line M and N read *ſit* inſtead of *ſit in detrimentum.*

¶ The Piæ Cantiones rhythmical form of the melody is the development of many years. For much intereſting information on this matter ſee the Rev. W. H. Frere's valuable and learned Notes on 'Hymns, Ancient and Modern' (1909), p. 76. Even in a mutilated form, the Tune has already enjoyed in England a popularity of more than half a century. It appeared firſt in the enlarged edition of the 'Hymnal Noted' in 1854, and thence paſſed into many other collections. It was ſaid to have been taken from a MS. at Wolfenbüttel of the twelfth century; but in the Preface to his 'Sequentiæ ex Miſſalibus' (1852), p. ix, Neale gives a complete liſt of the MSS. and early printed books, all of the fifteenth and ſixteenth centuries, that he examined on his viſit to the library of that place in 1851:—Pſalters, Miſſals, Hymners, and Books of Hours, but he makes no mention of this particular MS. Moſt probably it was Piæ Cantiones, 1582, which ſupplied him with this melody.

But however popular it may be, it has never received full juſtice; for from the firſt unwarrantable liberties have been taken, (i) with the rhythm and time; (ii) a melody ſet in Piæ Cantiones to *ſix* lines trochaic (7.6.7.6.7.6), has been marred by being miſ-metred and lengthened into a ſtanza of *ſeven* lines (8.7.8.7.8.7.7.). In other words, the meaſure of *Corde natus ex parentis* (Of the Father ſole begotten) is not the metre of *Diuinum myſterium.* A good attempt has been made by the Rev. R. P. Ellis ('Songs of Syon,' 1910, No. 133) to provide Engliſh words, beginning 'Unity in Trinity,' fulfilling the requirements of the Tune. But to be heard to full advantage, it has to be ſung to its Latin words as noted in Piæ Cantiones. For a much older, but far leſs pleaſing, form of the melody (one of nine collected and collated by the Rev. H. M. Banniſter), ſee the Rev. W. H. Frere's Notes aforeſaid.

XXI. Jesvs Christvs nostra salvs. ¶ 'Carmen nobile de venerabili ſacramento' (Cod. Labacen. 147, ſec. xv). 'Kirchengeſeng, darin die Heubartikel Chriſtlichen Glaubens gefaſſet.' (Böhm. Br., 1566.) 'Johannes Huſſen Liedt; ungeacht das er nun ketzeriſch war, hat er doch ſein Meinung von dem hoch werdigen Sacrament des Altars

Catholifcher Weis gehalten; welches kann und mag in den Catholifchen Kirchen und Verfammlungen ficher gefungen werden,' etc. ❡ Dreves ('Analecta Hymnica,' XLV*b*, No. 125, p. 105) prints this 'Cantio Euchariftica' from four different MSS.: (i) Grad. Altovadenfe anni 1410 [A]; (ii) Cant. Viffegradenfe, fec. xv [B]; (iii) Orat. MS. Pollingenfe anni 1501, at München [C]; (iv) Cant. MS. Pragenfe in the Böh. Mus. at Prag, anni 1512 [D]; (v) Wackernagel, I, No. 367, prints it from a fifteenth century München MS. verfion [M]. See alfo Daniel, II, No. lx, p. 370; Dreves, I, pp. 22, 31, 43, etc., and Julian, pp. 598 and 1657. The following are older readings than PIÆ CANTIONES:

St. I, l. 2, C reads *quam* for *quod*; and (if Dreves is to be trufted) in l. 4, B, C, and D read *dedit in* carnis *hoftiam*, but A has *panis* (Dreves, I, Anhang ix, p. 192).

St. II, l. 2, ABCD have *Tu folus es, Jefu Chrifte*, and *quo nunquam maius inuentum*.

St. III, D has *Virtus eft Euchariftia*, and l. 4, *Communionis gloria*, evidently a mifreading of *gracia*.

St. IV, ABCD are faid to read *Ave* pietatis *forma*; BD invert the order of *forma* and *norma*. They alfo read *qui te fide fpeculatur*.

St. V, M and A read *Non es panis fed es deus*, but BCD have *non eft panis fed eft deus*.

St. VI, l. 2, B and D read *inconfumens fit mutatus*.

St. VII, l. 2, M reads *pietatis dux fanctorum*.

St. VIII, ll. 3 and 4, B reads *Tibi fit laus et gloria | per infinita fecula*. L. 4, other MSS. read *duc nos vbi lux eft eua*; Daniel, *l. c.*, has authority for *duc nos vbi eft lux tua*.

St. IX is wanting from PIÆ CANTIONES as well as from C; but, to complete the Acroftic, the verfe *O quàm magna tu fecifti* is fupplied from the old MSS. D reads *dum te cruci impreffifti*; M, *qui te Chrifte, impreffifti*; B prefers *panis, vini in fpeciem*; M and D *vini et panis fpecie*; M has *apparentum* for *obfantium in facie*.

St. X (omitted in B and C); M, A, and D read *Caro cibus, fanguis vinum | eft myfterium diuinum*. At the end of this *Cantio* the Bohemian books add the following refrain,

235

refrain, unknown to Piæ Cantiones, *Eya iubilantes* | *vultum attollite* | *nostro creatori* | *symphonijs hymni-* *dicis* | *christum zelate.*

❡ 'Betreffs des Liedes, *Jesus Christus, nostra salus,* ist viel für und gegen diskutiert worden, ob Joh. Hus der Verfasser sei: das Akrostichon dürfte den sicheren Aufschlag geben.' Blume, 'Anal. Hymnica,' vol. xxix, p. 14.

❡ The Piæ Cantiones melody is in the Dorian mode, for the earliest form of which see the Hohenfurth MS. (Graduale Altovadense of 1410), as given in 'Anal. Hymnica,' I, Anhang, No. ix, p. 192; see Zahn, No. 1576, Meister, I, No. 278 ; but in Klug (1535) and elsewhere there is an entirely different melody, and certainly inferior to the P. C. air. The latter has been harmonized by the following musicians amongst others:

(i) Joh. Walther, as No. xxiv in his 1524 edition (and as No. lxxi in 1551) for three voices; also as No. xxiii in the same edition (this being No. xxvii in 1537, No. xxxvi in 1544, and No. xxxix or xli in 1551).

(ii) Seth Calvisius ('Harm. Cant. Ecclesiasticarum,' 1598), No. l, à 4; B. Gesius (1601), p. 63, à 5.

(iii) Balthasar Resinarius, *c.* 1543 (see Breitkopf, Band XXXIV, No. lv, à 4).

(iv) Joachim Decker in Gabriel Husduvius' 'Melodeyen GB' (1604), No. xliiii, à 4.

(v) Michael Prætorius, Part III (Helmstadt, 1607), No. iv, à 8.

(vi) Michael Prætorius, 'Mus. Sion.,' V (1607), No. cxxviii, à 4; No. cxxix, à 5.

(vii) Michael Prætorius, 'Mus. Sion.,' VII (1609), Nos. xci, xcii, xciii, and xcv (Braunschweig, Meissen, Schwa- bian, and Franconian forms respectively).

(viii) Joh. Hermann Schein, Cantional, 1645, No. lxxxix, p. 174.

(ix) Joh. Crüger (i) in his 'Geistl. Kirchen-Melodien' (1649), No. 104, für Stimmen, Violinen, und Cor- netten; (ii) in 'Praxis Piet. Mel.' (1656), No. 268, melody and bass.

(x) Samuel Scheidt (1587-1654), 'Tabulatura Nova.' See Breitkopf, 'Denkmaeler,' Band I, Th. 3, p. 217, No. 18. For organ, *sub communione.*

236   D. Buxtehude

(xi) D. Buxtehude (1637-1707), Breitkopf, Band II, No. 15;
'Motetten, Choräle und Lieder,' No. 41.

(xii) Friedr. Wilhelm Zachow (1663-1712), Breitkopf, Band
XXII, No. 28, p. 352, Organ Fugue in D minor.

(xiii) Joh. Pachelbel (1653-1706), Breitkopf, Band IV, Zweite
Folge, No. 42, p. 110 (*Bicinium*).

(xiv) Joh. Seb. Bach (i) No. 30 in his '371 Vierstimmige
Choral-gesänge.' (ii) Orgel Werke, Band II, p. 136,
sub communione, Pedaliter; and p. 140 *alio modo*.
(iii) Breitkopf, Orgel Musik, Band VIII, No. 108,
p. 116, in D minor; No. 109, p. 122, in E minor;
No. 110, p. 126, in E minor; and No. 111, p. 128,
in F minor. See also the 'Bach Gesellschaft' publication (Leipzig, 1889), No. 110.

(xv) Fridrich Layriz (1854), No. 67.

¶ In 1854 this Piæ Cantiones tune appeared in the
'Hymnal Noted.' It was there set to English words beginning 'In our common celebration.' This was a translation, by Dr. Neale, of a fifteenth century Sequence,
Omnes una celebremus, which latter is to be found in Clich-
toveus' 'Elucidatorium,' in Neale's 'Sequentiæ' (1852), in
Daniel, V, p. 216, and in Kehrein, p. 133. (See Julian,
pp. 868 and 1684.) But, to accommodate the tune of *Jesus
Christus nostra salus* to words of a different metre, unpardon-
able liberties were taken with it. For an English translation
of Joh. Hus' hymn, based on that of R. F. Littledale, in the
'People's Hymnal' (1867), beginning 'Jesus Christ our
blest Redeemer,' and capable of being sung to its proper
tune, see 'Songs of Syon' (1910), No. 141. It is main-
tained by no less an authority than Zahn that the first three
lines of this hymn are to be considered as trochaic, and
the last line iambic. ¶ In the Erfurt 'Enchiridion' of
1524, *Jesus Christus nostra salus* appears in the German as
*Jesus Christus unser Heiland | der von uns den Gottes Zorn
wandt;* 'gebessert,' as it is asserted, by Luther; but *Huius
contrarium verum est.*

XXII. O REX CŒLORVM DOMINE. ¶ Here called *Cantio
Precum*, and consisting of six stanzas of eight lines; but in
Gall Morel's 'Lateinische Hymnen des Mittelalters' (this
being a supplement to Mone, Daniel, and others) of the year

1868, it is described as *De Passione Christi,* and consists of six-
teen stanzas of four lines. Morel (No. 97, p. 64) prints it
in full from an Hymner, or Book of Hours, of the fifteenth
century, which he discovered at Einsiedeln. To judge from
the third stanza of PIÆ CANTIONES, it would seem to have
been composed by one who describes himself as *Theophilus,*
a sometime heretic (*Tu pius es hæretici misertus et Theophili*).
The Einsiedeln MS. [E] differs considerably from Petri of
Nyland's version, and reads in

Stanza II, Tu enim *pientissimus de superorum sedibus* venisti
me redimere; noli *redemtum* perdere [E].

Stanza III, In domo quondam Symonis | *mulieri plenæ*
criminis | tu *delesti* facinora | mira *tua* clementia.
Tuque pius hæretici | misertus *es* Theophili | : quia
conversus doluit | summam mercedem *meruit* [E].
The order of Stanzas III and IV is inverted in P. C.

Stanza IV, *Quod dignatus es dicere;* sed *pænitentem* viuere;
ad te, *redemtor,* clamito [E].

Stanza V, *Et pietatis vnicæ; sume preces quas offero; quis*
nisi tu me audiet? . . . subueniet? Si non ad te [E].

Before Stanza VI the Einsiedeln MS. has the following five
quatrains: (i) O pia dei genitrix, | virgo inestimabilis, | lepra
tabente criminum | ora pro me ad dominum. (ii) Tu es
regina omnium | et intacta post vinculum: | per te est data
omnibus | salus in te sperantibus. (iii) O Michäel arch-
angele | princeps celestis curie | cum turba sac fidelium |
habere refrigerium. (iv) Patriarcharum cunei | et prophet-
arum numerus | cum omnibus apostolis | delete noxam
sterilis. (v) Vos sancti dei martyres | confessores et virgines |
rogo in vestra requie | me consortem ascribite.

Stanza VI, Sit tibi laus et gloria | Jesu per cuncta secula|
qui misereris omnium | ad te *corde* clamantium.

❡ PIÆ CANTIONES' altered version has been reprinted by
Klemming, II, p. 62, but he inadvertently omits the O, and
starts with *Rex cælorum Domine. O Rex celorum Domine*
appears as *O Herre Gudh aff Himmelrijk* in Rhezelius (1619),
p. 267. Nowhere to be found in Dreves. ❡ The tune is
in the Dorian Mode, harmonized in 'Songs of Syon' (1910),
No. 414 B.

XXIII. AVE REGINA OMNIVM. ❡ In PIÆ CANTIONES this
begins

begins *Ave rex regum omnium* and comes under the head of *Cantiones precum*. For reasons already mentioned above in the Preface to this book, pp. x-xii, there was no alternative but to restore the words to their original form. This task has been accomplished with the aid of Dreves, XLV*b*, No. 184, p. 152. Klemming, II, p. 55 (1886), reprints Petri's version, which, to fall into line with the 'new learning,' had been altered for the worse. Here will be found Petri's variations from the original:

Stanza I, Ave *rex regum* omnium, *O Jesu*; *qui* for *quæ*.

Stanza II, l. 3, tu *solus*. The words of this stanza are meaningless when applied to our Lord.

Stanza III, l. 2, *O Jesu pie*, for *Maria piè*.

On p. 14 of vol. XLV*b*, Dreves remarks: 'Wer diesen Gallimathias im Zusammenhange lesen will, kann diesem Wunsche bei Klemming, II, pp. 33, &c. Genüge leisten.' ❡ The melody is in the Dorian mode. It may be sung to English words beginning *Jesu, the Father's Son and Heir*; harmonized in 'Songs of Syon' (1910), No. 346.

XXIV. SALVE, FLOS ET DECOR ECCLESIÆ. ❡ In PIÆ CANTIONES as a Christmas Carol. Reprinted by Klemming, II, p. 48. The form given in the present edition (1910) is taken from Dreves, XLV*b*, No. 183, p. 151, who rightly gives it as a *Marien-lied*. The following are Petri's variations from the older version:

Stanza I, l. 2, *Jesu Christe pie | patris in palatio*; l. 4, *lexq vitæ tuæ*; l. 6, *purum*; l. 7, *virgo sine viro peperit te | et post virginem declarauit se*; l. 8, Dreves has repeated *peperisti*, but it was a printer's error, and he clearly intended *permansisti* or *remansisti*; l. 9, *frater Jesu Christe*; l. 10, *qui cares*.

Stanza II, l. 1, *Hic adest*; l. 6, *pater*; l. 7, *hic scirpea fiscella*.

Stanza III, l. 1, *subleuator pie*; l. 4, *releuator pie*; l. 5, *rector*; l. 7, *pie*; l. 8, *director nostræ viæ*; l. 9, *et extremo die*.

❡ This also is a Dorian Mode melody. ❡ Set to English words (*Jesu, King of ages, prithee, hear us*) and harmonized in 'Songs of Syon' (1910), No. 339.

VIRGO

XXV. Virgo mater piissima. ❧ Another 'Carmen Marianum veteris ecclesie,' but appearing in Piæ Cantiones as one of his *Cantiones precum*, and beginning O *Christe rex pijssime*. The later version is given by Klemming, II, p. 59. Dreves' restoration (XLV*b*, No. 182, p. 151) has been adopted in this new edition of P. C. These are Petri's alterations, or those of his theological advisers:

Stanza I, 'O Christe rex pijssime | cunctorum plasmator- um, | tu nobis sis certissime | solamen peccatorum,' &c.

Stanza II, 'Hic sydus claritatis, Hic balsamo suauior,' &c. ❧ The melody is in the Phrygian Mode. For the sake of this tune, in 1854, Neale published his admirable *The World itself keeps Easter Day*' ('Carols for Easter-tide,' No. XIV), but the music was incorrectly rendered, the law of the ligature notes not being understood, and the last line of each verse was faulty, 'ăllĕlūĭă, ăllĕlūĭă' not being exactly the metrical equivalent of 'stŭpēndĭūm lăbōrĭs' | 'fĕruōrĕ chārĭtātĭs' | *or* 'ĭn vnĭtătĕ trĭnā.' These slight oversights have been attended to in 'The Cowley Carol Book' (1902), No. 50.

XXVI. Psallat fidelis concio. ❧ Reproduced by Klemming, II, p. 41. ❧ Here again preference has been shown for the older unreformed version as given in 'Anal. Hymnica,' XLV*b*, No. 180, p. 148. Petri had allowed the following alterations:

P. 38, last line but one, *Carmen nato Mariæ.* P. 39, l. 1, *quem sine labe criminis*, *ex pura carne virginis*; l. 9, *O nate ex puerpera.* P. 40, l. 3, *flos iuuenum* ; l. 4, *in serijs* ; l. 7, *beate* ; *nate diua* ; *sine spina* ; l. 8, *prælate.* P. 41, l. 7, O *Christe, salus.* P. 42, l. 5, *Tu natus es ex filia.* P. 43, l. 2, *Natus Dei Patris.* P. 44, l. 1, *veræ saluationis.* P. 45, l. 2, O *Pater pietatis.*

❧ The rule of Strophè and Antistrophè has been occa- sionally disregarded; and several stanzas are missing. ❧ For the varying strains of this sequence, Neale wrote *A Song, a Song our Chief to greet*, 'Carols for Easter-tide' (1854), but the music in certain places failed to correspond with Piæ Cantiones. See 'Songs of Syon' (1910), No. 108.

XXVII. AVE MARIS STELLA, DIVINITATIS. ❡ In PIÆ
CANTIONES this occurs as a Carol for Christmas-tide.

(A) Here are the PIÆ CANTIONES' words (copied by
Klemming, II, p. 13):

(1)   Ave maris stella, Diuinitatis cella,
      Natus castitatis, radix sanctitatis,
      Filius æternæ claritatis.
℟. Apparuit, apparuit,
      Quem pia virgo genuit Maria.
(2)   Aue puer mitis, süauitatis vitis,
      Mundi es creator, simul & saluator,
      Tu es omnis bonitatis dator.   Apparuit, etc.
(3)   Hodie saluator & angelorum sator
      Mitis & deuotus, in Judæa notus
      Nascitur & languet vt ægrotus.   Apparuit, etc.
(4)   Pannis inuolutum, quem virgo profert nudü
      Bos cognouit esse de radice Iesse,
      Quem Propheta cecinit expresse.   Apparuit, etc.
(5)   Umbra vetustatis, ænigma cœcitatis
      Transit, & in lucem virgo profert nucem,
      Dans Israël ex Ægypto ducem.   Apparuit, etc.
(6)   Ecce conceptura natumq paritura,
      Virgo nominatur atq salutatur,
      Mundus sic de morte liberatur.   Apparuit, etc.
(7)   Clamat Esaïas: iam præparate vias,
      Semitas & rectas Domino perfectas,
      Animas qui coronat electas.   Apparuit, etc.
(8)   Rigor perit legis, dum pro peccato gregis
      Pastor immolatur, hostia mactatur,
      Populus in tenebris saluatur.   Apparuit, etc.
(9)   Puer singularis, O Christe, stella maris,
      Salus in procella, nate de puella,
      Dominum pro nobis interpella.   Apparuit, etc.

(B) In the body of this book, p. 45, the older version of
Ave maris stella, diuinitatis cella naturally comes first, for it
may be traced back to a MS. of the thirteenth century,
bound up in an Antiph. MS. from St. Lamprecht (Codex
Græcen. 258), see Dreves, XX, p. 28, as well as p. 143. It
was desired to give both versions, old and new, exactly as
they stand. With the exception of the 9th stanza, P. C.
version is extremely good. ❡ The melody is in the
Phrygian mode. In 'Carols for Easter-tide' (1854), No. xv,
and in 'The Cowley Carol Book' (1902), No. 48, it is set
in four-pt. harmony to Neale's *Let us tell the Story.*

XXVIII. AVE MARIS STELLA, LVCENS. ❡ Of Bohemian origin. Dreves ('Anal. Hymnica,' I, No. 4, p. 49), gives five MSS. containing this *Cantio*: (i) The Hohenfurth MS., anni 1410 [A]; (ii) A MS. of the first half of the sixteenth century in the Böhm. Mus. at Prag [B]; (iii) Another Prag MS., VI, c. 20, of the fifteenth and sixteenth centuries [C]; (iv) The 'Graduale von Jistebnicz,' beginning of the fifteenth century; (v) Univ. Libr. Prag MS. X. E. 2, beginning of the sixteenth century [E], to which PIÆ CANTIONES (1582) must be added [P]. Reprinted by Klemming, II, p. 15. Dreves' form is given in this book. The variants are as follows: Stanza I, l. 5, *pons*, ABP; l. 7, *fons*, ABP; l. 8, *obumbratione*, CD. Stanza II, l. 3, *probleuma*, B; l. 6, *De Moab aduersum ens*, B; l. 9, *in te nostra rata spes*, BE. Stanza III, l. 5, *manans ros*, BEP; l. 9, *positus sub patris ir*' (i.e., *sub patris ira*), P; but the other MSS. read *nec in cuius ponit ir*. Dreves thinks that the meaning requires *sed* (or *et*) in cuius ponit ir, etc. *Ir* is a Græcism; *Ir* or *hir* (neuter gender noun, and indeclinable) is the Latin way of writing XEIP, hand. Our Lady is the *rubus quem non urit pyr*, the bush unburnt by fire, Exod. III, 2, 3, and under whose care, in whose hand the heavenly Man-Child placed himself; see Jeremiah, xxxi, 22, 'a new thing, a woman shall compass a man.' PIÆ CANTIONES spoils the metaphor by transferring 'the unburnt bush' to our Lord himself, and reads *positus sub patris ir*', i.e., placed under the Father's wrath; but it is neither usual nor allowable even in Monkish Latin to write *ir*' short for *ira*. Mone, II, No. 498, p. 22, lines 177-180, quotes a similar use of *ir* from a Reichenau MS. of the fifteenth century at München: *Natus ex te, dia | dulcis O Maria | te in hierarchia dextro locat ir.* ❡ For this PIÆ CANTIONES melody Neale expressly wrote his *Earth to-day rejoices* ('Carols for Christmas-tide,' 1853, No. V), and thence it was embodied as No. 6 in 'The Cowley Carol Book' (1902). It is hard to define the Tonality of this Carol, for, though having the Phrygian cadence, it sounds more like a Lydian, or Hypo-Ionian, strain.

XXIX. VANITATVM VANITAS. ❡ Apparently first found in PIÆ CANTIONES. Reprinted by Klemming, IV, p. 5, and thence drafted into Dreves, XLV*b*, No. 190, p. 157.

Chevalier

Chevalier adds that it occurs also in Hauréau, in 'Journ. d.
Sav.' (1888), p. 29. As the initial letters of the last three
stanzas end respectively in A V S, Dreves wonders whether
it may not have formed part of a lost acrostic. ❡ For this
tune, in 'Carols for Easter-tide' (1854), No. xiii, and in
'The Cowley Carol Book' (1902), No. 47, Neale wrote
his *Let the merry Church bells ring*.

XXX. INSIGNIS EST FIGVRA. ❡ Reprinted by Klemming,
IV, p. 22, and Dreves ('Anal. Hymnica,' XLV*b*, No. 192,
p. 159). ❡ For the tune (in the Dorian Mode) set to
original English words and harmonized, see 'Songs of Syon'
(1910), No. 403.

XXXI. MIRVM SI LÆTERIS. ❡ For a reprint from PIÆ
CANTIONES, see Klemming, IV, p. 31, and 'Anal. Hymnica,'
XLV*b*, No. 188, p. 156. On page 54, St. II, l. 4, *O mundi
Sophia* is probably an alteration of *O virgo Maria*, which
the words *pro nobis dominum | iugiter implora* seem to re-
quire. ❡ The melody is in the Dorian Mode. Set to the
words *Life is full of trouble*, and harmonized as No. 405 in
'Songs of Syon' (1910).

XXXII. O MENTES PERFIDAS. ❡ Klemming, IV, p. 41;
and Dreves, XLV*b*, No. 194, p. 160. Strangely enough
the first four lines of this *Cantio* also occur in the midst of
a *Planctus Marie Virginis*, as 4th stanza there. See Dreves,
XX, No. 198, p. 155, where it is part of a Sequence, taken
from a Troper MS. of the thirteenth century (Cod. Stuttgartien., HB, I, Asc. 95). The *Planctus* begins *Flete, fideles
animæ*, but, with the exception of verse 4, there is nothing
in common between this MS. and PIÆ CANT. ❡ The
melody is again in the Dorian Mode. In 'The Cowley
Carol Book' (1910), No. 59, it is harmonized and wedded
to English words, *Ye heav'ns, uplift your voice*.

XXXIII. MVNDANIS VANITATIBVS. ❡ Reprinted by Klemming, IV, p. 35, and thence by Dreves, XLV*b*, No. 191,
p. 158. ❡ In Stanza III, last line, Dreves suggests *fruuntur*
instead of *funguntur*. ❡ A Dorian Mode melody.

XXXIV. Honestatis decvs iam mvtatvr. ¶ Another
song *De temporum iniquitate*. Klemming, IV, p. 29; and
Dreves, XLV*b*, No. 195, p. 161. In Stanza I, laſt line but
one, Dreves rightly reads *metas* for Petri's *ætas*, repeated.
¶ The melody is in the Phrygian Mode.

XXXV. Scribere proposvi. ¶ Printed in E. du Méril's
'Poéſies Populaires Latines,' p. 125, from a Paris MS., B. R.
fonds de Notre-Dame, No. 273 bis, fol. 120, dated A.D. 1267.
This in ſix ſtanzas [D]. Alſo in Dreves, XXI, No. 150 (i)
from a Trop. MS. Dublinenſe, ſec. xiii, Cod. Cantabrigien.
Add. 710, in ſeven ſtanzas [C]; (ii) from Cod. Montis
Serrati, ſec. xv, in nine ſtanzas (Dreves, XXI, No. 151) but
with conſiderable variations and with quite a different refrain
from *Surge, ſurge vigila* [M]. Only verſes 1, 4, and 5 of
Piæ Cantiones correſpond at all with the Monte Serrato
form, while the latter has ſeveral ſtanzas peculiar to itſelf.
The following are the variations:

Stanza II, l., *in hoc mundo vixere* [C]; l.2, *venies ad tumulos*
[CD]; *ſi vis eos quærere* [C]; l. 3, *carnes computruere*
[CD].

Stanza III, l. 1, *In hac vita naſcitur* [D]; ll. 2, 3, et in
vitam ducitur | humano cum labore | et poſt vitam
[D].

Stanza IV, l. 1, *breuitas* for *breviter* [D]; *Mors venit*
[CDM]; l. 2, Omnia mors perimit [DM]; cunctaque
m. p. [C].

Stanza V, found only in Piæ Cantiones. Stanza VI,
miſſing in D; l. 1, *quam felices fuere* [C]; l. 2, *cum
ipſum adſpectabunt* [C]; l. 3, Sanctus, Sanctus Sabaoth |
Oſanna conclamabunt [C]. Here the likeneſs to
DCM ceaſes. ¶ Two additional ſtanzas from C
and D ſeem worthy of a place here:

    I (a) Tela fit araneæ præſentis mundi vita:
          labilis et flebilis non eſt in tuto ſita:
          labitur et flectitur nunc (?) eſt exinanita. [D]

    I (b) Tela ſic araneæ eſt mundi præſens vita;
          labitur et frangitur, non eſt in tuto ſita,
          labilis et fragilis nunc eſt inexanita. [C]

    II (a) Si conuerſus fueris et velut puer factus, (ſanctus, MS.)
          et vitam mutaueris in meliores actus,
          ſic intrare poteris regnum Dei beatus. [D]

II (b) Si conuerſus fueris, nunc quaſi puer natus,
et a tuis vitijs animo purgatus,
tunc fruique poteris regno Dei beatus. [C]

❡ Many verſes of a ſimilar character occur in Du Méril,
and in Thomas Wright's 'Latin Poems,' commonly attributed to Walter Mapes (London, 1841). It ſeems poſſible
that this Walter Mapes, or more properly Map (c. 1140-
1210), may have been the author of 'Scribere propoſui.'
See Du Méril's intereſting footnote on p. 125 of his
'Poéſies populaires Latines.'

❡ Piæ Cantiones verſion is given by Klemming, IV,
p. 16. ❡ The tune is written in the Æolian Mode; but
ſome would conſider it a Dorian melody. ❡ It was well
harmonized by the Rev. T. Helmore, as No. XXIII in
'Carols for Eaſter-tide,' 1854, ſet to the Rev. J. M. Neale's
'Twas about the dead of night; alſo it occurs in 'The Cowley
Carol Book,' No. 52. ❡ In vol. XXI, p. 220, Dreves gives
another melody in the Phrygian Mode, from the above-
named Cod. Montis Serrati, fifteenth century: but, as
uſual, the Piæ Cantiones tune is much to be preferred.

XXXVI. Mars præcvrrit in planetis. ❡ Reprinted
by Klemming, IV, p. 14, and copied thence by Dreves,
XLVb, No. 198, p. 163. ❡ Hora nouiſſima, tempora peſſima
ſunt is the burthen of this ſong. ❡ The P. C. tune is
adopted by Rhezelius (1619), p. 300, ſet to the words En
farligh tijdh nu kommen år. ❡ The laſt verſe, Jeſu Chriſte,
fili patris, has been tranſlated as Jeſu, Son of God the Father,
and is ſet to its proper muſic, as No. 345, in 'Songs of
Syon' (1910). ❡ The melody is in the Hypo-Ionian
Mode.

XXXVII. Invalvit malitia. ❡ Klemming, IV, p. 12,
whence it was copied by Dreves, XLVb, No. 199, p. 164.
❡ In the laſt line of the laſt ſtanza, P. C. reads niſi ipſa
vita; but, to ſupply the miſſing ſyllable, and to enable it to
be ſung correctly, the liberty has been taken of reading
ipſius inſtead of ipſe. Dreves, however, ſuggeſts ſuperna.
❡ Tune in the Dorian Mode.

Cvm

XXXVIII. Cvm sit omnis caro fœnvm. ⁋ Formerly
afcribed to St. Bernard of Clairvaux, but latterly to Philippe
de Grève (†1236). It is found in the Egerton thirteenth
century MS. 274 in the Britifh Mufeum, f. 27, verfo.
There it confifts of three ftanzas, the fecond of which, not
included in Piæ Cantiones, runs thus: Per etatum incre-
menta | immo magis detrimenta | ad non effe traheris, |
ficut umbra cū declinat | uita fugit & feftinat | claufa meta
funeris. Two other MSS. quoted by Dreves, XXI, No. 142,
p. 95, one of the thirteenth century at Firenze, and the other
from the Miff. Aquilegienfe (1508), contain the following
lines not contained in Piæ Cant. (i) 'O fors grauis, O fors
dura | , O lex dira, quam natura | promulgauit miferis,'
and (ii) 'Ergo cum fcis qualitatem | tuæ fortis, voluptatem |
carnis quare fequeris?'

⁋ In ftanza I, laft line, P. C. varies from the other books
by reading *qui de terra fueris* for *qui de terra fumeris*; and in
ftanza II, l. 3, it improves the rhyme by reading *fimilis efficeris*
for *fimilis effeƈtus es*. For further information fee Julian, p.
1627 (i). The P. C. verfion is reproduced in Klemming, IV,
p. 3.

⁋ In 1854 Neale wrote his *Eafter-day comes on but flowly*,
No. XXIV in his 'Carols for Eafter-tide,' but the mufic was
incorreƈtly given. Beginning with Neale's fecond ftanza, *Of
the hour that comes to fever*, it occurs as No. 49 in 'Songs of
Syon' (1909), the mufic-note agreeing with P. C. and harmonized by the Rev. G. H. Palmer. The Melody is in the
Phrygian Mode. ⁋ Egerton MS. 274 gives an entirely
different (Dorian) tune. Dreves profeffes to have copied
the Melody from this Egerton MS., but if fo, inaccurately:
cf. 'Anal. Hymnica,' XXI, p. 214.

XXXIX. Castitatis specvlvm. ⁋ Reprinted by Klemming, IV, p. 45, and thence copied into 'Anal. Hymnica,'
XLV*b*, No. 202, p. 166. ⁋ St. II, l. 3, *Lucretiæ natus*, as
already obferved above in the preface (p. xi) is a charaƈter-
iftic fpecimen of the bad tafte of the Renaiffance, and its
affeƈtation of claffical paganifms. 'The Son of Lucrece,' *i.e.*
Jefus, fon of Mary. Elfewhere Our Lady is ftyled 'Diana';
but, on the other hand, the ufe of Olympus and Tartarus for
heaven and hell, may be found in the beft Ambrofian Hymns.

St.

St. V. *Tabulatis calceis* seems to mean 'in long pekyd schon,' 'in pointed shoes.' *Tabulatus* signifies 'tabulated' or 'boarded.' Perhaps, 'like Chess, or Backgammon boards.' At backgammon we still speak of making up our *points,* as having 'good or bad *tables.*' In Joh. Lichtenberger's

'Prognosticatio' (Quentel), Cöln (1526), there is a remarkable wood-cut—the representation of a young fop in the act of being stript of his secular garments, having his hair shorn, and his long-piked shoon shortened with a pair of scissors. In the foreground of the picture, which is here reproduced, may be noticed dice and playing-cards, while his chess and

backgammon

backgammon boards, the 'points' of which latter closely re-
semble the former shape of the young man's shoes, are already in flames. The wearing of 'piked shoon' was a con
tinual source of minor trouble to the authorities of the
Medieval Church. On the other hand, some suppose *tabulatis calceis* to mean shoes of 'chequered-pattern,' or perhaps
'with high heels.'

In St. VI, last line, Dreves reads *vt* for *et*; but the latter
makes equally good sense and grammar.

❡ The Melody is probably in the Hypo-Ionian Mode,
for which see 'The Cowley Carol Book' (1902), No. 55,
where it has been harmonized by Mr. B. Luard Selby, and set
to English words, *Holy Church must raise the lay*, a free translation of an eleventh-century sequence beginning *Carmen suo
dilecto*.

Stanza II, page 67. *Boëtij studia.* The following passage
seems to be here referred to: 'Quid autem de corporis volup-
tatibus loquar, quarum appetentia quidem plena est anxie-
tatis, satietas vero poenitentiae? Quantos illae morbos, quàm
intolerabiles dolores quasi quendam fructum nequitiae fruen-
tium solent referre corporibus! Quarum motus quid habeat
iucunditatis ignoro. Tristes vero esse voluptatum exitus,
quisquis reminisci libidinum suarum volet, intelliget. Quæ
si beatos explicare possunt, nihil causæ est, quin pecudes
quoque beatæ esse dicantur quarum omnis ad explendam
corporalem lacunam festinat intentio.'—*Phil. Consol., III*, 7.
p. 64. Rud. Peiper, Lipsiæ, 1871.

XL. O SCHOLARES DISCITE. ❡ Dreves ('Anal. Hymnica,'
XLV*b*, No. 201, p. 165) reprints Klemming, IV, p. 58,
but fails to take notice of the earlier readings, quoted by
Klemming, from 'Cod. vetus Wadstenensis J. VI, quartus in
ordine, nunc Vpsalensis 32.' As Klemming is itself a somewhat rare book, and as this Upsala MS. [V] is overlooked
by Dreves, the PIÆ CANTIONES version has been collated
with the older MS.; and the variations are here recorded.

Stanza IV, l. 3, [V] reads *faciunt* for *adigunt*; ll. 7, 8,
    Quid *eò flebilius | si tu, rex propicius, mittas vltionem?*
    Stanza V, l. 1, [V] reads Regula *claustralium* for
scholarium (cloisters having made way for schools).
    Stanza VI, l. 3, [V] reads *Omnia pertranseo ita quod*

non

non video; l. 5, *vos eſtis in ſtudio*; l. 6, *lite confidentes.*
Stanza VII, [V] reads *Qui in terris proprium | vobis
patrimonium | dedit ſpiritale,* which ſeems to require
an inverſion of the order of the firſt two lines.

¶ *Jeſu, who in bitter pain,* No. 62 in 'The Cowley
Carol Book' (1902), ſupplies original Engliſh words and
harmonies to the Piæ Cantiones Melody, which is apparently written in the Hypo-Ionian mode.

XLI. Scholares convenite. ¶ Klemming, IV, p. 69,
'Anal. Hymnica,' XLV*b*, No. 200, p. 164. ¶ Stanza III,
l. 2, the *Quinterna* is the zithern or guitar. The Statutes of
the Academy of Vienna in Auſtria rule: 'Scholares non
vacent magis tabernæ, dimicaturæ, aut *quinternæ,* quam
Phyſicæ aut Logicæ ſeu ſacræ Facultati.' 'Let not the
Scholars ſpend more time in the tavern, in tuſſling, or at the
guitar, than over their Phyſicks, Logick, and Divinity.' See
Du Cange, 'Gloſſarium,' V, p. 1077. *Quinternizare* is to
play the cittern. ¶ The air is in the Phrygian ſcale.

XLII. Disciplinæ filivs. ¶ Klemming, IV, p. 48;
'Anal. Hymnica,' XLV*b*, No. 206, p. 168. ¶ St. III,
l. 1, *Quid nocet id perdere,* etc., ſeems to refer to St. Matt.,
x, 39, 'He that loſeth his life for my ſake ſhall find it.'
Line 2, *Quidnam cutem vendere* is built on 'Satan's old
ſaw' in Job, ii, 4, 'Skin for ſkin, all that a man hath will
he give for his life.' Cf. Horace, Ep. I, ii, 29, and his
'*curare cutem,*' to take care of one's ſkin, to make much of
oneſelf. St. IV, l. 1, *Dulcia non meminit qui non guſtat
triſtia*: cf. Boët, 'Conſ. Phil.,' II, pr. 4, 'In omni aduerſitate
fortunæ, infeliciſſimum eſt genus infortunij fuiſſe felicem.'
Cf. alſo S. Thom. Aq., 'Sum. Theol.' II, ii, 36, 1, 'Memoria
præteritorum bonorum . . . in quantum ſunt amiſſa, cauſat
triſtitiam'; and Dante, 'Inf.' v, 121, 'Neſſun maggior dolore|
Che ricordarſi del tempo felice | Nella miſeria.' But here
Diſciplinæ filius is recommended firſt to drink of the bitter
cup, that the honey may taſte all the ſweeter afterwards,
in the recollection of the paſt, for l. 2, *Mel (ut Plato cecinit)
ſapit poſt abſynthia.* For the following note we are indebted
to the Regius Prof. of Greek in the Univerſity of Cambridge,
Dr. Henry Jackſon, Fellow of Trinity College. He writes:

'I

'I cannot remember anywhere in Plato the equivalent of the *illuſtration*, "Mel ſapit poſt abſynthia." Moreover, according to Aſt's Lexicon, the words ἀψίνθιον and ὄξος (vinegar) do not occur in Plato. But you have an equivalent for the general ſentiment—'Dulcia non meminit qui non guſtat triſtia'—in 'Phædo,' 60, 13: ὡς ἄτοπον, ἔφη, ὦ ἄνδρες, ἔοικέ τι εἶναι τοῦτο, ὃ καλοῦσιν οἱ ἄνθρωποι ἡδύ· ὡς θαυμασίως πέφυκε πρὸς τὸ δοκοῦν ἐναντίον εἶναι, τὸ λυπηρόν, τῷ ἅμα μὲν αὐτὼ μὴ ἐθέλειν παραγίγνεσθαι τῷ ἀνθρώπῳ, ἐὰν δέ τις διώκῃ τὸ ἕτερον καὶ λαμβάνῃ, σχεδόν τι ἀναγκάζεσθαι λαμβάνειν καὶ τὸ ἕτερον, ὥσπερ ἐκ μιᾶς κορυφῆς συνημμένω δύ' ὄντε.' ('How ſingular is the thing called pleaſure, and how curiouſly related to pain, which might be thought the oppoſite of it: for they are never preſent to a man at the ſame inſtant, and yet he who purſues either is generally compelled to take the other; their bodies are two, but they are joined by a ſingle head')—tr. by B. Jowett, 'Plato's Dialogues,' vol. II, p. 198. Chaucer here is much to the point:

> For how might ever ſweetneſſe be knowë
> To him that never taſted bitterneſſe?
> [Troilus and Criſeyde, Book I, ll. 638-9.]

St. IV, l. 3, *Nam Mattheus concinit*, etc. The paſſage alluded to is apparently St. Matt., x, 28, 'But rather fear him who is able to deſtroy both ſoul and body in hell.'

❡ The Melody is in the Ionian mode.

XLIII. IN STADIO LABORIS. ❡ Klemming, IV, p. 52, and Dreves, XLV*b*, No. 187, p. 155. ❡ 'Give me neither poverty nor riches' (Prov. xxx, 8) is the burthen of this ſong. ❡ This remarkable Melody (in the Dorian mode) and charming metre inſpired Neale to write *The Morning of Salvation* (No. XX in his 'Carols for Eaſter-tide' (1854, and harmonized by the Rev. T. Helmore). Thence it was adopted by 'The Cowley Carol Book' (1902), No. 49.

XLIV. SCHOLA MORVM FLORVIT. ❡ Klemming (IV, p. 66) 'Anal. Hymnica,' XLV*b*, No. 207, p. 169. But the Editor of the laſt-named volume has overlooked ſeveral printer's errors. In St. I, it ſhould be *mox*, inſtead of '*mos* timore defluo'; in St. II, *inſtruxit* is given inſtead of *inſtruit*; and in

St. V, *funt* inftead of *fint*. ❡ The Melody is in the Phrygian mode. Unfortunately, the PIÆ CANTIONES mufic is alfo incorrectly printed on page 174 of the above volume of 'Anal. Hymnica.'

XLV. SVM IN ALIENA PROVINCIA. ❡ Klemming, IV, p. 71, prints this *Cantio* with feveral older readings taken from the Codex vetus Wadftenenfis MS. 32, now at Upfala.

In Stanza IV, laft line, this MS. reads, *Sed fum unus pauper ftudens*; in Stanza V, laft line, *iam factus fum ut aratro*. ❡ Dreves, XLV*b*, No. 208, p. 170, quoting PIÆ CANTIONES, begins thus, *Aliena provincia*. On page 174, his rendering of the PIÆ CANTIONES Melody, in the firft two lines, is again very far from accuracy. ❡ The Melody is in the Dorian mode, harmonized in 'Songs of Syon,' No. 414C. ❡ The Latin words require care in finging, for there are feveral redundant fyllables in the third and fifth verfes as well as in the firft. But if the Mafter of the Quire will only underftand that this is a 'Long Metre' compofition, he will have little or no difficulty in difpofing of the extra fyllables. The falfe accents of Stanza IV, Milés effém, équitaffém, etc., and the ftrange liberties taken with the fecond, Per té, Deús nos fáluauit, et á morté libérauit, will fhock the ear of the claffical fcholar.

XLVI. O SCHOLARES VOCE PARES. ❡ An invitation to the dance and banquet. See Klemming, IV, p. 63; Dreves, XLV*b*, No. 209, p. 170. Mentioned by T. Norlind, p. 16. ❡ For Neale's words, *Days grow longer, funbeams ftronger*, fee 'Carols for Eafter-tide' (1854), No. XIX, and 'The Cowley Carol Book,' No. 58. ❡ The Melody is in the Eighth Gregorian mode, *i.e.*, the Hypo-mixo-lydian. Dreves, XLV*b*, p. 174, gives the mufic-note correctly.

XLVII. O QVAM MVNDVM, QVAM IVCVNDVM. ❡ On Peace and Concord. Klemming, IV, p. 76; Dreves, XLV*b*, No. 203, p. 167. ❡ In the Ionian mode, that is, the Modern Major Scale of C. It may be found harmonized and fet to Englifh words in 'The Cowley Carol Book,' No. 29.

XLVIII. LÆTEMVR OMNES SOCIJ. ❡ Klemming, IV, p. 75;

251

'Anal. Hymnica,' XLV*b*, No. 204, p. 167. ❡ The Melody is in the Æolian mode.

XLIX. ZACHÆVS ARBORIS ASCENDIT STIPITEM. ❡ A Church Dedication Festival *Benedicamus Domino*, here labelled 'historical' because it tells the story of Zaccheus. It is of Bohemian origin, appearing in Dreves, I, No. 147, p. 149. It is found (i) in the 'Graduale von Jistebnicz' of the beginning of the fifteenth century, a MS. in the Böhm. Mus. at Prag. [D]; and (ii) in MS. X.E.2 of the beginning of the sixteenth century, in the Univ. Libr. also at Prag. [E].

In Cod. Bruxellen. 8860-67, sec. x initio, there occurs at the end of a hymn, 'Zachæus per fidem | ascendit arborem | ut transeuntem | videret Dominum' (Dreves, XII, No. 2, p. 14).

In Stanza III of PIÆ CANTIONES, the older MSS. read *Illique pandens* instead of *Illic perpendens*, which latter is probably corrupt. In Stanza V, l. 1, PIÆ CANTIONES follows the ' Jistebnicz Gradual,' D, while E reads *Ergo de tali*. Between the first and second verses of PIÆ CANTIONES the Bohemian MSS. both insert two distichs: (A) *Jesus dum transiens sursum respiceret | Zachæo imperauit ut descenderet.* (B) *Zacchæe, festinans descende huc ad me | Quia in domo tua volo manere.* E gives no Doxology. D has a different one from PIÆ CANTIONES, viz., *Laus tibi sit et honor sancta trinitas | , Deo dicamus infinitas gracias.*

❡ The setting for two voices is ingenious and pleasing; quoted by T. Norlind, p. 18, as an interesting example of an early Carol in Rondo form. ❡ Klemming, IV, p. 92.

L. HOMO QVIDAM REX NOBILIS. ❡ Klemming, IV, p. 87; 'Anal. Hymnica,' XLV*b*, No. 186, p. 154. ❡ Parable of the Great Supper in verse (St. Luke, xiv, 16-24). Petri classes it amongst his 'Cantiones Historicæ.' In a modern reprint (Stockholm, 1862) of a Swedish Psalmboken of 1536 there is to be found a faithful translation of *Homo quidam rex nobilis* in this metre, and, like PIÆ CANTIONES, in fourteen stanzas, beginning, *En riker man, wellogher han.* It occurs, also in the vernacular, in ' Then Swenska Psalmeboken' of

1572, fol. liiii. Rhezelius (1619), p. 264, directs that a Carol
beginning *En lijknelse klar | och uppenbar* is to be sung
'under the Nother: *En riker man | weldigh år han*'; *i.e.*,
to the tune of *Homo quidam rex nobilis*. ❡ It may be sung
to Neale's original English words, *Give ear, give ear, good
Christian men* ('Carols for Easter-tide,' 1854, No. XVI), but
there the music is incorrectly given; and in 'The Cowley
Carol Book' (1902), No. 45, to be brought into conformity
with Piæ Cantiones, the last two bars require revision.
❡ The Melody is written in the Hypo-Ionian mode.

LI. In vernali tempore. ❡ Klemming, IV, p. 81;
'Anal. Hymnica,' XLV*b*, No. 210, p. 171. In spite of
Petri's Preface, '*Quamuis interim negari non possit, cum omnia
hæc rythmica potius sint quàm poetica*,' etc., this lyric alone
(in praise of Spring time) proves that he took an extremely
modest view of the poetical beauty of at least one of the
contents of his book. ❡ In 1853 Neale wrote his admirable
Christmas Carol, No. X, *O'er the hill and o'er the vale*, but
again the music was misunderstood. In 'The Cowley Carol
Book,' No. 16, the necessary corrections have been made.
❡ This is a fine example of an Hypo-Dorian mode Melody;
it is copied without mistake in Dreves, XLV*b*, p. 175.

❡ It is on record that Herr Otto Goldschmidt and
Madame Goldschmidt (*née* Jenny Lind, a Swede) were in
the habit of having carols sung in their house in London
several times in the year. On the Feast of the Epiphany
they made a point of singing *O'er the hill and o'er the vale*
to this lovely Piæ Cantiones Melody.

LII. Tempvs adest floridvm. ❡ Klemming, IV, p. 83;
'Anal. Hymnica,' XLV*b*, No. 211, p. 171. ❡ The Melody
(in the Hypo-Ionian mode) in Rhezelius (1619), p. 142, is
set to Swedish words: *Then lustige tijdh nu år*. For this
Piæ Cantiones tune Neale wrote his now well-known *Good
King Wenceslas look'd out*, 'Carols for Christmas-tide' (1853),
No. XI. In the above-named volume of 'Anal. Hymnica,'
p. 176, in the last bar of the last line C and F should be
semibreves, not minims. ❡ On p. 88, first stanza, l. 3, it is
probable that the rel. pronoun *quæ* had been omitted between the words *Gramina & plantæ* and *hyeme quiescunt*.

SVPPLEMENTVM

⁋ It is to be noticed that hitherto many of the Piæ Cantiones Melodies [from I-LII] have been purposely transposed, for reasons already notified in the Preface of this Book. Those, however, that follow in the Svpplementvm [except LIII, LV and LXXIII], are printed each in their original Clef. It was originally intended to publish only a selection of Petri's Piæ Cantiones, and those which were easiest; but later on it was decided to reprint all. This is the Editor's apology for the size of this Supplement.

LIII. De radice processerat. ⁋ Reprinted from Piæ Cantiones in Klemming, II, p. 18; and in 'Anal. Hymnica,' XLV*b*, No. 168, p. 135. ⁋ In the second line of the refrain, 'Flos Christus est,' 'Anal. Hymnica' wrongly reads *veraciter* for *suauiter*. In St. II, in the phrase, 'Hoc est corpus meum,' 'meum' is *extra metrum*. ⁋ Apparently a Lydian mode Melody with B moll.

LIV. Lætetvr Iervsalem. ⁋ Klemming, II, p. 31; 'Anal. Hymnica,' XLV*b*, No. 164, p. 133. ⁋ In St. I, l. 4, Dreves wrongly reads, 'natus est à filia,' repeating and making 'filia' rhyme with 'filia' in l. 2; in St. II, l. 3, he alters Piæ Cantiones *mitigatur* into *irrigatur*. ⁋ The tune (in the Ionian mode) is printed as it stands (G on the middle line). In Rhezelius (1619), p. 48, the tune is set to the Swedish words, *Frögde sigh Ierusalem*.

LV. Avtor hvmani generis. ⁋ Klemming, II, p. 74; 'Anal. Hymnica,' XLV*b*, No. 175, p. 140. ⁋ On p. 96 *exsoluit quæ non rapuit* is an echo of a similar phrase in 'Cedit hyems eminus' (No. XVII above, p. 24), *soluit quæ non rapuit*. ⁋ Several misprints of Dreves ought to be here noticed. In the above volume of 'Anal. Hymnica,' in St. I*a*, on p. 140, he reads *mirabilis* instead of *mirabili*; on p. 141, St. I*b*, he reads 'vitæ veræ perfice, nos *aspice*,' instead of 'vitæ veræ perfice nos *apice*'; in St. 3*b*, he needlessly suggests (*re*)*quies* for *quies*; in St. 5*a*, he reads *dignis lucis dotibus* instead of *dignis locis, dotibus*; and in 6*a*, *pertinacia* for *peruicacia*. ⁋ The Melody is in the Ionian mode, or the Lydian

mode, with B moll, transposed. ❡ In free imitation of this
sequence (for such it really is), Neale wrote *The foe behind,
the deep before*, No. XXII in 'Carols for Easter-tide' (1854).
He began in the middle of 'Autor humani generis,' starting
at the words 'Sic morte mortem destruis,' page 102. Neale's
words have been much admired, but have had no chance
of being heard to full advantage, for again the Melodies of
Piæ Cantiones were misinterpreted, the law of the ligature
being misunderstood, so that the above-named setting in
'Carols for Easter-tide' cannot honestly be recommended.

❡ In Hymns, Ancient and Modern (1904), No. 159,
part of *The foe behind* has been correctly given, so far as it
goes; except that in the music of the third bar on page 253
(H. A. and M.), the ligature is, for once, disregarded. But
a comparison with Piæ Cantiones, and with 'Carols for
Easter-tide' (1854), will show that several of the most
beautiful refrains of the music in the latter part of this
Cantio, besides some of the very best of Neale's words, have
been, for some reason, unfortunately omitted.

LVI. A dextris dei Dominvs. ❡ Klemming, II, p. 70*b*;
'Anal. Hymnica,' XLV*b*, No. 171, p. 137. Considered by
Dreves as *De Natiuitate Domini*, but in Piæ Cantiones *De
Passione Domini*. ❡ For another and shorter form of this
Cantio see 'Anal. Hymnica,' XX, No. 120, p. 104. This
is taken from Cod. Maihing. (ol. Kirchenheimen.), II, 2, 8°
13, sec. xvi [M]. Of its three stanzas only the first and third
at all correspond with Piæ Cantiones. In St. I, M reads
initio qui sedet; and in refrain 'Rosam spina parit' M's reading, *expers pœnæ*, is much to be preferred before Piæ Cantiones *sanctam uerè*, which latter fails to rhyme with *fluunt
venæ* and *dicat benè*. For further variations see 'Anal.
Hymnica,' XX. ❡ The tune, in the Phrygian mode, is
printed here, as in Piæ Cantiones, in the Tenor Clef.

LVII. Amoris opvlentiam. ❡ Klemming, II, p. 71;
'Anal. Hymnica,' XLV*b*, No. 174, p. 139. In St. I, the
latter reads *et exsul*, instead of *vt exul*. ❡ The Melody
is chiefly remarkable for its wide range beyond the strict
limits of the Dorian mode; and also for its much synco-
pation.

LVIII. ÆTAS CARMEN MELODIÆ. ❡ The words are re-printed by Klemming, II, p. 81. ❡ An interesting specimen of early three-part writing. The Discantus is written in the Alto Clef, the lower part in the Barytone Clef. All three parts sound melodious.

LIX. CEDIT HYEMS EMINVS. ❡ Transposed into the G Clef, the Tenor part of this *Cantio* has already appeared in the previous part of this work, see No. XVII. No. LIX may be considered as affording a *locus pœnitentiæ*, where the Tenor is restored to its proper Clef, with the addition of the Discantus and the Bassus. The latter contains the original *Canto Fermo*, which, however, gradually made way for the more melodious Tenor. In 1531 the Bass had not yet been ousted, but by 1582, as proved by PIÆ CANTIONES, it had undergone some modifications, probably for contrapuntal consideration's sake. In Germany it is known as *Weltlich Ehr und zeitlich Gut*. For Michael Weisse [geburtig von d'Neisse], and older versions of this Bohemian air, see Zahn, VI, p. 11; also III, No. 4971 *a* and *b*. For other two- and four-part settings see Zahn, Nos. 4973-5, including one by M. Prætorius (1609), where the old Bass Melody has dis-appeared. In 1619, Rhezelius, p. 94, prints the Tenor only, exactly as it stands in PIÆ CANTIONES, but ignores the Bass. Joh. Seb. Bach has taken the Tenor as a fresh Melody, and harmonized it accordingly. See his ' 371 Vierstimmige Choralgesänge,' No. 211.

LX. IVCVNDARE IVGITER. ❡ See above, No. XVIII, where, on the assumption that the chief Melody lay in the Tenor, the latter only was printed, but transposed, for convenience' sake, into the G Clef. Here, however (No. LX), will be found the Descant and Bass as well as the Tenor, all in their original Clefs. It is possible, after all, that the principal Melody is borne by the Bass. All the parts are written in the Dorian Maneria, authentic or plagal.

LXI. IESV DVLCIS MEMORIA. ❡ A Cento, consisting of three stanzas of five lines apiece, rhyming *aabbb*, from the well-known Hymn generally attributed to St. Bernard of Clairvaux (1091-1153); see Julian, pp. 585 (ii), 1536

256   (ii),

(ii), and 1656 (ii). 'But Dom. Pothier has found this hymn, in MSS. of the eleventh century, ascribed to a Benedictine Abbess; so St. Bernard's claim to the authorship, always a doubtful one, is now disproved' ('Revue Grégorienne,' X, p. 147). [Frere in 'H., A. and M.' (1909), p. 356.] ❡ St. III of PIÆ CANTIONES is corrupt. It reads, *Jesu mi essentiam*, but in the present work it has been restored to '*Jesu, mi bone, sentiam*, for which there is good authority. ❡ Lovers of old-fashioned polyphonic music of the sixteenth century are at liberty to write and print these four parts in close score, and hear how they sound. But it must be confessed that for *Jesu dulcis memoria* more pleasing melodies and settings than these might easily be found. ❡ The *Canto Fermo* is apparently in the Tenor; a Dorian mode Melody.

LXII. O DVLCIS IESVS. ❡ A fragment of some Passion-tide or Easter Sequence. Dreves ('Anal. Hymnica,' XLV*b*, No. 179, p. 147, footnote) considers that it was, accidentally or purposely, inserted in 'Laus Virginis' (see No. LXVII of the present work), coming immediately before the words *Eya, solari facie* (p. 158). The Sequence having been restored to its original form, by the aid of Dreves, it seemed best to remove these words, which, as testified by the music, were out of place in the middle of 'Laus Virginis,' and to print them here separately. ❡ Unlike the words, the Melody is part of 'Laus Virginis.' It belongs to the Dorian mode.

LXIII. QVANDO CHRISTVS ASCENDERAT. ❡ Lucas Lossius, in his 'Psalmodia, *hoc est*, Cantica Veteris Ecclesiæ' (1553), p. cxviii, informs us that this was a 'Benedicamus, correctum per Hermann: Bonnum,' *i.e.*, by Hermann Gude, of Lubeck, Lutheran. ❡ For the text see Lossius (1561, 1569, and 1579), also Wackernagel, I, p. 281. ❡ For the tune refer to Lossius, 1561 and 1569 editions, p. 136; 1579 edition, p. 144; or Zahn, II, No. 2581. It is a Phrygian mode Melody.

LXIV. [BENEDICITE] TRES PERSONAS TRINITATIS. ❡ Klemming, II, p. 2, Dreves ('Anal. Hymnica,' XLV*b*, No. 172, p. 138) points out (i) that 'Das Lied ist ein s.g. *Benedicite*, d.h. ein Tischgebet für das gemeinschaftliche Weihnachts-

mahl der clericuli'; (ii) that it really begins with the words
Tres perſonas Trinitatis. ❡ The Melody is in the Æolian
mode, or the Firſt mode (Dorian) tranſpoſed.

LXV. BENE QVONDAM DOCILES. ❡ Klemming, II, p. 3;
'Anal. Hymnica,' XLV*b*, No. 178, p. 144. ❡ The acroſtic
ſpells the Author's Chriſtian name: BIRCERVS. Poſſibly
Bircerus Gregorij, Abp. of Upſala (1366-83), author of
many hymns, *e.g.,* 'Dies ſalutis agitur' (in honour of St.
Birgitta), 'Botuidi laudes colere,' 'O turris fortitudinis,'
'Vale, robur debilium,' quoted by Klemming, I, pp. 21, 58,
and 59, of his 'Hymni, Sequentiæ et Piæ Cantiones' (1885),
copied from the 'Strengnäs Breviary,' Stockholm (1495).[1]
❡ Notice that the laſt line of every ſtanza is, or elſe pro-
feſſes to be, a perfect Hexameter. PIÆ CANTIONES text is
not always to be truſted; for inſtance in St. II, l. 4, it reads
Affirmarunt, when *affirmant,* as pointed out by Dreves, is
the right word; St. III, l. 1, the acroſtic would be ruined
if *Vident* is to be read inſtead of *Rident*; St. IV, l. 4, the
order of the words *pariter* and *ſunt* is inverted; in St. VI,
l. 4, the reading of *Verum Deus* for *Sed Deus* makes the
Hexameter, already bad enough, worſe than ever; in St.
VIII, l. 4, *nos* after *puros* is redundant. ❡ A Phrygian mode
Melody.

LXVI. FLORENS IVVENTVS VIRGINIS. ❡ For Petri's 'corrected' verſion of this Song in honour of our Lady ſee
PIÆ CANTIONES itſelf, or Klemming's reprint thereof, II,
p. 23. In the preſent work the older form, reſtored by Dreves
in 'Anal. Hymnica,' XLV*b*, No. 163, p. 131, has been
chiefly adopted. In PIÆ CANTIONES *Florens iuuentus virginis*
falls under the heading of 'Cantiones de Natiuitate Domini.'
❡ The following are Petri's alterations: on p. 139, l. 4,
virum for *viro,* but either is good Latin; p. 140, l. 2, *qui* for
quæ; p. 141, l. 5, *portum* for *portus*; and p. 142, l. 1, Petri
reads *ſpem* for *ſpes,* and l. 5, *et ſchola*; Dreves, *eſt ſchola*;
p. 143, l. 1, Petri reads *ſcientiam* and *rhetoricam,* where Petri
has *ſcientia* and *rhetorica*; alſo, l. 2, Petri reads *hunc* for

[1] More compoſitions of Bircerus Gregorij are to be ſeen in 'Anal.
Hymnica,' XXV, p. 181; XXXVII (?), No. 151; XLII, No. 192;
XLIII, Nos. 167, 174 and 175.

hanc;

hanc; l. 5, *Christe, nate ex domina*, instead of *O sanctissima domina*; p. 145, l. 1, *ductor gregis* and *doctor legis*; p. 146, l. 2, *orans* for *ora*, where the imperative is required; p. 147, l. 3, *pater misericordiæ*; p. 149, l. 3, *et melodum*, where Dreves prefers *ut melodum*.

❡ The Melody is in the Ionian mode. On p. 173 of the same volume of 'Anal. Hymnica' Dreves prints the first few pages of the PIÆ CANTIONES Music; but these abound in mistakes.

LXVII. LAVS VIRGINIS. ❡ As restored by Dreves ('Anal. Hymnica,' XLV*b*, No. 179, p. 145). For PIÆ CANTIONES 'corrected' form see the Book itself, or Klemming's reprint, II, p. 33. These are P. C.'s alterations: p. 150, l. 2, *natus carens*, thus spoiling the rhyme, as demonstrated by *totis votis* below; p. 151, l. 3, *prædestinatus* for *prædestinata*; l. 4, *sanctus* for *sancta*; *ortus* for *orta*; *præcognitus, qui*, and *præditus*, masculine for feminine. Page 152, l. 5, *Sophia* for *Maria*; p. 153, l. 1, *hora* for *orta*; also *regem tuum patrem*, which fails to rhyme with *et rosarum milia*, but *regem nati filia* does. P. 154, l. 3, *tu es virtutum* for *tu es virtutis*; p. 156, l. 5, *O sancta domina* rhymes with *tu nostra nomina*, but not so with *O nate Mariæ*; p. 157, l. 1, *Patri commenda* in lieu of *Nato commenda*; l. 8, *qui dignitatis*, instead of *quæ dignitatis*; p. 158, l. 3, *O dulcis Jesus* was here wrongly inserted after the words *tenes arcem cælorum* [see notes on Cantio LXII supra]; l. 3, *splendens nate regina*; p. 159, l. 1, *fili regis* instead of *mater regis*; *sis dux gregis*; l. 6, *Patri Domino*; p. 160, l. 1, *qui te dedisti pretium*; l. 2, *da quoque in te*; p. 161, third line, Dreves reads, *Christo*, P. C., *Christi*. ❡ P. 156, l. 4, Petri reads *Joel* for *Jael*. ❡ The varying strains of this *Cantio* (Dorian mode) are no less beautiful than the words.

LXVIII. VNICA GRATIFERA. ❡ For the Revised Version of this *Cantio*, 'improved' by some professor of the 'new religion,' see PIÆ CANTIONES (1582), repeated by Klemming, II, p. 49. The 1910 edition follows the old version, as restored in 'Anal. Hymnica,' XLV*b*, No. 181, p. 149. The following are Petri's alterations of the older work: p. 163, l. 1, *Christe rosa* for *virgo rosa*; l. 5, *gaude, Christe mirabilis* for *gaude, mater mirabilis*; p. 164, l. 10, *pater misericordiæ*; p. 165,

l. 8,

l. 8, *caste* for *casta*; *domine* for *domina*; p. 166, ll. 6, 8, the order of the lines *pium patrem ostende* and *ab hostibus defende* is inverted; *patrem* is substituted for *matrem*. ❡ This *Cantio* is also set to a series of melodies, all in the Dorian mode.

LXIX. Paranymphvs adiens. ❡ Of Bohemian origin. ❡ Klemming, II, p. 40, reprints the Piæ Cantiones version. For an older form, taken from the Prag. MS. VI, B. 24, of the first half of the sixteenth century, see 'Anal. Hymnica,' I, No. 43, p. 83. This MS. varies from P. C. in the following ways: by reading in St. I, *adijt* for *adiens*; *nymphulæ* for *nymphale*; St. III, *Psallat ergo* concio | *tota cleri cum iubilo* | *nato regi neophico*. ❡ The two-part setting is in the Phrygian mode. But according to Dreves ('Anal. Hymnica,' I, p. 199, No. XXV) these two melodies are written in the Dorian mode.

LXX. Parce virgo spes reorvm. ❡ Piæ Cantiones, copied by Klemming, II, p. 60, had greatly altered this ancient 'Carmen Mariale.' This is how it stands in the above-named books:

St. I.   Parce Christe spes reorum pœnitenti seruulo
         ipsum soluens à suorum delictorum vinculo,
         Potes enim quantum velis: ergo parce Domine
         Ad quid namq te fidelis si careret crimine
         inuocaret? nec tu fores tantò dignus solio
         ni fuissent peccatores & Patrum transgressio
         Etsi pœnam culpa poscit, culpam delet gratia
         cum sit maior qui ignoscit, quàm is cui sit venia.

St. II.   Iveundare gloria: reis vena veniæ
         Iesu Christe, cæcis via, fons & dator gratiæ
         huc intende, condescende pijs quæso precibus
         ac faueto vultu læto meis supplicatibus
         Dei Nate, Fili grate Patris qui te fecerat.
         Nunc Natura sua iura mutare stupuerat
         Christe frater, tua mater virgo viri nescia.
         Stella solem parit prolem, cuius erat filia.

❡ The heresy concerning our Lord's Divinity in St. II, l. 5 (already alluded to on p. xii of our Preface), made it impossible to ask orthodox Christian people to sing or say the above Piæ Cantiones version. So, instead thereof, we give the more correct form of *Parce virgo*, found by Dreves in

Cod. Taurinen. Reg., 11 (ol. S. Jacobi Leodien.), fec. xiii;
fee 'Anal. Hymnica,' XX, No. 218, p. 169.

❡ The Piæ Cantiones setting for two voices is apparently
written in the Phrygian and Hypo-Phrygian, the third and
fourth modes, transposed. According to Dreves, the aforesaid
Cod. Taurinen. contains a three-part setting of the same, or
of some other, tune.

LXXI. Nvnc floret mendacivm. ❡ Klemming, IV,
p. 38; Dreves, XLVb, No. 193, p. 160, but in St. II, l. 1,
the latter reads *suppeditatur* for P. C.'s *sub pede datur*, and
omits & before *vsura Sathanæ*, needlessly, for Petri has provided an extra note for this &. Dreves is of opinion that
three lines of words have been lost after *sensu abutuntur*.
❡ The Melody is written in the Æolian mode, or perhaps
in the Dorian mode transposed.

LXXII. In hoc vitæ stadio. ❡ Klemming, IV, p. 19;
Dreves, XLVb, No. 189, p. 157. ❡ 'Of the miseries of
this sinful world.' It must be noticed that each stanza con-
cludes with a tolerably good Hexameter, followed by a
Pentameter, in *Leonine verse*; *i.e.*, 'A kind of verse much
used in the Middle Ages, consisting of hexameters and pen-
tameters, in which the final word rimes with that immediately preceding the caesural pause. Prob. named from some
Mediæval poet called Leo (or Leonius) who made use of
this kind of versification : for conjectures as to his identity
see Du Cange.' (Murray's English Dict., Oxford, 1903;
vol. vi, p. 203, col. 2, under Leonine 2.) ❡ The Melody
is another example of the Phrygian scale.

LXXIII. Iam vervs amor expiravit. ❡ Klemming, IV,
p. 8; 'Anal. Hymnica,' XLVb, No. 197, p. 162, beginning,
'Verus amor exspirauit' (the initial *Iam* being omitted alike
in Strophè and Antistrophè). Dreves observes that the last
two stanzas but one, beginning *Maior cedit et obedit*, bear
strong resemblance to Stanzas III and IV of *Jeremiæ prophetiæ* (see No. LXXIV of this book). ❡ The Melody is
in the Phrygian mode.

LXXIV. Ieremiæ prophetiæ. ❡ Klemming (IV, p. 26),
nearly

nearly always correct, nevertheleſs here reads in St. I, *vox in Roma*, inſtead of *vox in Rama*. Dreves ('Anal. Hymnica,' XLV*b*, No. 196, p. 162) remarks that St. III and IV alſo occur towards the latter end of *Iam verus amor expirauit* (ſee No. LXXI, above). ❡ The plainſong of this two-part ſetting (in the Dorian mode) is ſuppoſed to lie in the Baſs.

LXXV. Olla mortis patescit. ❡ *Ad clerum.* ❡ Klemming, IV, p. 54; 'Anal. Hymnica,' XLV*b*, No. 205, p. 168. ❡ The acroſtic ſpells Olavvs. The thirteenth Abp. of Vpſala was Olaus *ſapiens* († 1333), ſee Eric Benzelius' 'Monumentorum,' p. 40; the ſame authority mentions Olaus Laurentij (magnus rhetor), the twentieth Abp. of Vpſala († 1438); while Dreves ſuggeſts Olaus Magni, Bp. of Åbo († 1460); but Olaf was an extremely common name. ❡ In St. II, laſt line, Dreves reads *aræ ſe vult dicare*, inſtead of Petri's better reading *ære ſe vult ditare.* ❡ The tune is in the Dorian mode.

LXXVI. Regimen scholarivm. ❡ Klemming, IV, p. 65. Text not printed in Dreves, but in 'Anal. Hymnica,' XLV*b*, p. 14, reference is given to Klemming, and this ſhort poem is deſcribed as being doubtleſs only a Torſo. *Regimen ſcholarium* is mentioned by T. Norlind ('Svenſk Muſikhiſtoria,' 1901, p. 18), in connection with the ſubject of Diſcantus and Organum. The laſt line, *Ut mea prædicta tanto non agmine victa*, is another inſtance of a Leonine Hexameter, ſee No. LXXIII above. ❡ The chief Melody (in the Dorian mode) is in the Baſs.

LXXVII. Ramvs virens olivarvm. ❡ Acroſtic, Ragvvaldvs. Reprinted by Klemming, IV, p. 93, and by Dreves, 'Anal. Hymnica,' XLV*b*, No. 85, p. 153. ❡ An hiſtorical *Cantio* in praiſe (i) of S. Henry, the Engliſhman, Abp. of Upſala, Ap. of Finland and Martyr; (ii) of S. Eric of Sweden, King and Martyr. ❡ Firſt, of S. Henry. Born in the early part of the twelfth century, he preached the Faith in Norway with his kinſman Nicolas Breakſpeare (afterwards, in 1158, Pope Adrian IV). After the conqueſt of Finland, King Eric determined to avenge himſelf on that country of pirates and freebooters, in no worſe way, however, than by teaching his new subjects the Christian Religion. For this difficult task Henry, Abp. of Upsala, was chosen. The conversion of the Finns followed, but it was purchased with the life-blood of S. Henry. So many of his successors, Bishops of Finland, received the crown of martyrdom that the saying arose *Episcopus in Finlandia non ad honorem sumptus, sed expositus martyrio reputatur*. S. Henry suffered on 19th January, 1151. His relics were had in veneration at Upsala until the Reformation, when they scattered to the four winds. Hymns, Invitatories, Antiphons, and Responds, taken from old Swedish MSS. and from early printed Service-books, may be found in Klemming, I, pp. 126, 127, 133, and 136; and in 'Anal. Hymnica,' XLII, Nos. 238 and 239; XLIII, Nos. 289-294. He is described as *ortus in Britannia; præsul insignis; patronus Finlandiæ*, etc. ❡ Next, of S. Eric, the ninth King bearing that name, and one of the Patron Saints of Sweden, worthy to be classed with S. Edward the Confessor, King of England, and with S. Louis, King of France. After a ten years' reign, he also fell a martyr to the Faith of Christ (18th May, 1151). His shrine remains to this day at Upsala, undefaced. Sacred poems in praise of this monarch may be seen in Klemming, I, p. 91, and in 'Anal. Hymnica,' XXV, No. 11, and elsewhere. He is described as *iustus; illustris; rex deuotus; Dei amicus; humilis; honestus; patiens; pius atque modestus*.

❡ It is comparatively well known that Germany owes much of her Christianity, under God, to the zeal and labours of British, Scottish, and Irish monks, such as SS. Boniface, Willibrord, Swibert, Burchard, Kilian, Willibald, Lullus, and others who, in the seventh, eighth, and ninth centuries, left the Western Isles to uproot Paganism and to plant the Cross in foreign lands. They went forth, with the love of Christ in their hearts, with their lives in their hands, and with the Songs of Holy Church on their lips. It is a matter of history that it was British monks who founded Bishoprics, Monasteries, Universities, and Quire-schools, *e.g.* at Aichstadt, Bobbio, Erfurt, Köln, Mainz, Nürnberg, Paris, Passau, Pavia, Regensburg, St. Gallen, Wien, and Wurtzburg. But it is not so fully recognized that the nations of Scandinavia—Norway, Denmark, and Sweden—are also indebted to Englishmen for their knowledge of the Catholick Faith.

Yet

Yet the old Swedo-Finnish Office-books record the names of some of the English missionaries who were instrumental in the conversion of that part of Europe:

(i) S. Sigfrid, of York, afterwards Bp. of Wexiö in Gothland († 1045). He is described as *Hic Anglicus angelicus; Anglie ortus | ut sydus Swecie | præclarum radiauit; Sigfridus, dictus signifer | et dei verus armiger.* The King of England Mildredus, *i.e.,* Edred, is requested by King Olaf to send over a teaching priest. Sigfrid volunteers to go. *Rex Mildredus aggregatis | Anglicanis tunc prelatis | querit, quis ad Swecie | esse velit de prefatis | patribus ecclesie | qui ad fidem trinitatis | ducat gentes in peccatis | datas ydolatrie.* And again Sweden thanks God, *qui Sigfridum his aduexit | oris olim ab Anglia.*

(ii) S. Dauid, Ap. of Westmanland. Of him it is recorded, *Hunc Anglia progenuit | claris ortum parentibus | qui veritatem docuit | Suecos dignis virtutibus;* that he was *piorum pius filius | parentum Dauid inclytus.* They inquire, What brought him to Sweden?

> ℟. Pater Dauid, stirpe clarus,
> vita iustus, arte gnarus,
> digna proles Anglie,
> cur venisti de remotis,
> in indoctis Suenis, Gottis
> viam vite querere?

His answer is,

> ℣. Vidi claras margaritas,
> licet luto delinitas
> iacentes in puluere;
> derelictis regno, patre,
> rebus charis atque matre,
> has volebam emere.

(iii) S. Eskill, Bp. and M., Ap. of Sudermanland, kinsman of S. Sigfrid of York (12th June, 1069). He is praised no less highly than SS. Sigfrid and Dauid; witness the following lines:

(a) Laudent Sudhermannie | pueri parentem | in prole Britannie | lapsos erigentem.

(b) Gaude, felix Suecia | laudans saluatorem | qui de Britannia | tibi dat pastorem.

(c) Gaude, parens Britannia, | de tante prolis munere | exulta magis Suecia | de nouo lucis sydere.

(d) Percussus est lapidibus | Eskillus sicut Steffanus.

O

(e) O proles Britannie | recta via morum | preful Sudermannie | tutor
orphanorum | te collaudat hodie | digne gens Suecorum | quam,
pater exime, ducas ad regna polorum.

These Saints were long commemorated in Sweden, 'quos
direxit Anglia | noftre falutis gracia | et quos produxit
Suecia | qui modo funt in gloria; | hos petimus humiliter |
et credimus ftabiliter | quod noftra fint refugia.'

❡ The lift of Britifh miffionaries might be eafily length-
ened by quoting the names of S. Ulfrid, Bp. and M. (28th
January, 1028), of Roduard, Richolf, Edward, Grimkell,
Rudolf, Bernhard, Thomas, and others, who, with S. Henry
of Upfala, were pioneers of Chriftianity in Sweden and
Finland. It ought to be more clearly underftood that it was
Britons who firft overthrew idolatry in thefe lands, who
built Chriftian Churches, not Academies of Science, but
Schools of Jefus Chrift. It was our fellow-countrymen who,
'by the innocency of their lives and conftancy of their
faith even unto death,' eventually tamed and won the
hearts of the favage people of Sweden, a country till then
over-run with ignorance, vice, and fuperftition, who taught
thefe barbarians to fing 'the Lord's Song in that ftrange
land.' Thefe were the fpiritual forefathers of the *Veteres
Epifcopi*, of whom Theodoric Petri, of Nyland, rightly fpeaks
in terms of the utmoft veneration—'fuch as found out mufical
tunes and recited verfes in writing.' PIÆ CANTIONES is in
itfelf fufficient witnefs to the influence and to the refults of
the teaching of thefe Britifh clergy men, who were fecond
to none in Europe in their love and knowledge of Plainfong
and Medieval Mufic, and of the capabilities and beauties of
the Gregorian Ecclefiaftical Modes. Of thefe ancient Finnifh Melodies, reinforced as they have been by contributions
from Germany, France, Poland, and Bohemia, it may be
prophefied that they will furvive, when much later-written
mufic fhall have perifhed. While to Petri himfelf, the com-
piler of PIÆ CANTIONES, the words of the old heathen poet
Callimachus (*c.* 260 B.C.) may not inappropriately be applied:

ἀλλὰ σὺ μέν που . . . τετράπαλαι σποδιή,
Αἱ δὲ τεαὶ ζώουσιν ἀηδόνες ᾗσιν ὁ πάντων
ἁρπακτὴρ Ἀΐδης οὐκ ἐπὶ χεῖρα βαλεῖ.

265   ('Although

('Although [Petri], methinks, thou thyself art long, long
time ago turned to duſt and aſhes, yet thy nightingale-notes
do ſtill live on. On theſe that ravager of all things, Death,
ſhall ne'er lay hand.')

LXXVIII. Magnvm nomen domini. ❡ This ought to have
appeared earlier in the book, as the concluding part of No.
III (*Reſonet in laudibus*); but, through an unfortunate over-
ſight, it was there omitted. However, *Magnum nomen Domini*
is often printed, by M. Prætorius and others, as a ſeparate
Cantio. Therefore, that nothing be loſt of Piæ Cantiones,
it is here printed out of place, with the recommendation
that it be ſung as a Carol complete in itſelf; or, better ſtill,
as a chorus to *Reſonet in laudibus*, and, anyhow, as a fitting
cloſe to Petri's admirable collection of ancient ſong.

> Laus, honor, virtus Domino,
> Deo Patri, et Filio,
> Sancto ſimul Paracleto!—Amen.

List of some of the Principal Works to which reference is made in the foregoing Explanatory
Notes

BAEUMKER [Wilhelm]. *See* Meister [K. S.]. Das katholische deutsche Kirchenlied, etc. Freiburg. 1862-1891. 3 vols.   [*Words and music.*

BOEHME [Franz Magnus]. Altdeutsches Liederbuch. Volkslieder der Deutschen nach Wort und Weise aus dem 12 bis zum 17 Jahrhundert. Leipzig. 1877.
[*Words and music.*

BREITKOPF AND HAERTEL. Denkmäler deutscher Tonkunst. Erste u. Zweite Folge. Leipzig. [Many vols.]
[*Music and often the words also.*

CAROLS FOR CHRISTMAS-TIDE. Set to ancient melodies by Thomas Helmore; the words by John Mason Neale. London. Novello. 1853.

CAROLS FOR EASTER-TIDE. Set to ancient melodies by Thomas Helmore. The words, principally in imitation of the original, by John Mason Neale. London. Novello. 1854.

CHEVALIER [Ulysse]. Repertorium Hymnologicum. Louvain. 1892-1904. 3 vols.
[*First lines of Hymns, with references.*

DANIEL [Hermann Adalbert]. Thesaurus Hymnologicus. Halis. MDCCCXLI-MDCCCLVI. 5 vols.   [*Words only.*

DREVES [Guido Maria] AND BLUME [Clemens]. Analecta Hymnica Medii Ævi. Fifty vols. 1886-1907.
See especially Vol. I [Cantiones Bohemicæ]; and Vol. XLV*b* [Cantiones Svecicæ, pp. 131-179].
[*Words; with Tunes occasionally.*

DU MÉRIL [ÉDÉLESTAND]. Poéſies populaires latines du moyen âge. Paris. 1847. [*No muſic.*

JULIAN [JOHN]. A Dictionary of Hymnology; Reviſed Ed. with New Supplement. London. Murray. 1907.
[*No muſic.*

KEHREIN [JOSEPH]. (i) Kirchen und religiöſe Lieder aus dem zwölften bis fünfzehnten Jahrhundert. [Anhang.] Paderborn. 1853. [*Words only.*

(ii) Katholiſche Kirchenlieder, Hymnen, Pſalmen aus den älteſten deutſchen gedruckten Geſang-und Gebet-büchern. 4 Bde. Würzburg. 1859-1865.

'*Die älteſte katholiſche Geſangbücher von Behe [Vehe], Leiſentrit, Corner und andern.*' [*No muſic.*

KLEMMING [GUSTAF EDVARD]. (i) Hymni, Sequentiæ et Piæ Cantiones in Regno Sueciæ olim uſitatæ. 1885. [KLEMMING I]. [*No muſic.*

(ii) Piæ Cantiones. S. Trinitas; Jeſus Chriſtus; S. Spiritus; S. Maria. Holmiæ. 1886. [KLEMMING II].
[*No muſic.*

(iii) Piæ Cantiones in Regno Sueciæ olim uſitatæ. SANCTI EXTERI. Collectionum noſtri æui Supplementum è fontibus Sveticis depromptum. 1887. [KLEMMING III].
[*No muſic.*

(iv) Latinſka Sånger från SVERIGES MEDELTID. Cantiones morales, ſcholaſticæ, hiſtoricæ in Regno Sueciæ olim uſi-tatæ. Holmiæ. 1887. [KLEMMING IV]. [*No muſic.*

MEISTER [KARL SEVERIN]. Das katholiſche deutſche Kirchenlied in ſeinen Singweiſen von den früheſten Zeiten bis gegen Ende des ſiebzehnten Jahrhunderts. Erſter Band. Freiburg im Breiſgau. Herder. 1862. Zweiter Band begonnen von K. S. Meiſter, und bearbeitet von Wilhelm Bäumker. Freiburg. 1883. Dritter (Schluſz=) Band. W. Bäumker. *Ibid.* 1891. [*Words and muſic.*

MONE [FRANZ JOSEPH]. Lateiniſche Hymnen des Mittel-alters, aus Handſchriften herauſgegeben und erklärt, etc. 3 Bde. Freiburg im Breiſgau. 1853-55. [*No muſic.*

NEALE [JOHN MASON]. (i) Hymni Eccleſiæ, à Breviarijs quibuſdam et Miſſalibus . . . deſumpti. London. 1851.
[*No muſic.*

(ii) Medieval

(ii) Medieval Hymns and Sequences. London. 1851. Second Edition, with very numerous additions and alterations. 1863. [*No muſic.*

NORLIND [Tobias]. Svenſk muſik hiſtoria. Helſingborg. 1901. [*No muſic.*

PRÆTORIVS [Michael]. Muſæ Sioniæ, I-VII. Publiſhed, either at Regenſpurg, Jehna, Helmſtadt, Hamburg (?), Noriberg, or Wolffenbüttel, between the years 1605-10. *See* Zahn, VI, p. 106, etc. [*Words and muſic.*

RHEZELIO [Haqvino Lavrentii A] *i.e.*, Haakon Laurencesen of Rhezel. Någre Pſalmer | Andelige Wijſor och Loffonger | vthſatte af Lavrentio Jonæ gestritio. Paſt. Hernöſand. Och nu med Noter affſatte | och aff Trycket vthgångne aff Haqvino Lavrentii A. Rhezelio Predikant i Grämuncka Clöſter. . . . Tryckt i Stockholm. 1619. [*Words and muſic.*

SONGS OF SYON. [George Ratcliffe Woodward.] Third Edition, reviſed and enlarged. 1910. London. Schott and Co. [*Words and muſic.*

THE COWLEY CAROL BOOK. [George Ratcliffe Woodward.] London. Mowbray. 1902.
[*Words and muſic.*

WACKERNAGEL [Carl Eduard Philipp]. Das deutſche Kirchenlied von der älteſten Zeit bis zu Anfang des XVII Jahrhunderts, etc. 5 Bde. Leipzig. 1862-77.
[*Text only.*

WINTERFELD [Carl von]. Der evangeliſche Kirchengeſang und ſein Verhältniſs zur Kunſt des Tonſatzes. 3 Th. Leipzig. 1843-47. [*Words and muſic.*

ZAHN [Johannes]. Die Melodien der deutſchen evangeliſchen Kirchenlieder, aus den Quellen geſchöpft und mitgeteilt von J. Zahn. 6 Bde. Güterſloh. 1889-93.
[*Firſt ſtanzas, firſt lines of words; and melodies, with many variations, occaſionally harmonized.*

General Index

271   Cant.

275

Alphabetical

Alphabetical Index of First Lines

Gaudete,

Paranymphus

CHISWICK PRESS: CHARLES WHITTINGHAM AND CO.
TOOKS COURT, CHANCERY LANE, LONDON.

THE PLAINSONG AND MEDIAEVAL MUSIC SOCIETY.

PRESIDENT.

The Right Hon. THE EARL OF DYSART.

The Society is founded for purely antiquarian purposes, with the following objects :—

1. To be a centre of information in England for students of Plainsong and Mediaeval Music, and a means of communication between them and those of other countries.

2. To publish fac-similes of important MSS., translations of foreign works on the subject, adaptations of the Plainsong to the English Use, and such other works as may be desirable.

3. To form a catalogue of all Plainsong and Measured Music in England, dating not later than the middle of the sixteenth century.

4. To form a thoroughly proficient Choir of limited numbers, with which to give illustrations of Plainsong and Mediaeval Music.

The subscription for Members is £1 per annum, entitling them to all publications *gratis*. Clergymen and Organists are eligible for election as Associates, at a Subscription of 2/6 per annum, which will entitle them to the annual publications at a reduced price. For List of Publications see next page.

PUBLICATIONS OF THE SOCIETY.

Price, stric
N>

THE MUSICAL NOTATION OF THE MIDDLE AGES *(out of print)*

SONGS & MADRIGALS OF THE 15th CENTURY, containing fourteen specimens, with *fac-similes* and rules for translating the music into modern notation (Quaritch) ... ... £1.6.

GRADUALE SARISBURIENSE, a *fac-simile* of a 13th Century English Gradual, with an introduction giving a history of the development of the *Gradale* from the *Antiphonale Missarum* of St. Gregory, with elaborate Indexes to the Offices, Graduals, etc., and to works on Liturgiology. The volume contains 102 pages of Text and 293 pages of Collotypes, and represents the most important part of the Ecclesiastical Music of the Middle Ages (Quaritch) *(out of print)* ...

THE SARUM GRADUAL, being the introduction to the GRADALE SARISBURIENSE, with four *fac-simile* pages (Quaritch) ... 15/9

ANTIPHONALE SARISBURIENSE, a *fac-simile* of a 13th Century English Antiphoner. This work, when complete, will be uniform with the *Gradale Sarisburiense*, and will contain over 700 pages of Collotypes. It is being published in yearly parts. Parts I to XII, now ready, with portfolios, price ... ... £12.12.

EARLY ENGLISH HARMONY, from the 10th to the 15th Century. Vol I., containing 60 Collotype Plates of music by composers from St. Dunstan down to John Dunstable (Quaritch) ... ... £1.6.

The above works are folio and on thick paper.

MADRIGALS OF THE 15th CENTURY, containing six Madrigals in modern notation, *quarto* (Novello) *(out of print)* ... ...

BIBLIOTHECA MUSICO-LITURGICA, a descriptive hand-list of the Musical and Latin Liturgical MSS. of the middle Ages preserved in English libraries. *Fascicle* I. and *Fascicle* II., making Vol I., *quarto*, 164 pp. with 13 *facsimiles* (Quaritch) ... ... £1.5.6.

THE ORDINARY OF THE MASS, *édition de luxe* (Quaritch) ... 7/10

PLAINSONG HYMN-MELODIES & SEQUENCES, *édition de luxe* (Quaritch) 7/10

RECENT RESEARCH IN PLAINSONG, *édition de luxe* 3/3

The above editions consist of numbered copies to which the issue is limited.

ELEMENTS OF PLAINSONG 2/9

A GENERAL OUTLINE OF PLAINSONG ... ... 3d.

WAGNER'S INTRODUCTION TO THE GREGORIAN MELODIES
A Handbook of Plainsong 5/4

St. GREGORY & THE GREGORIAN MUSIC 2/8

WHY USE PLAINSONG (12 copies) ... ... 4d.

*CHOIR RESPONSES ... ... 3d.

DEPRECAMUR TE (as sung by St. Augustine and his companions) ... 3d.

*THE PSALM TONES & OFFICE RESPONSES ... ... 4d.

ORGAN ACCOMPANIMENT to the Psalm Tones 2/9

Organ accompaniments can be obtained in MS. from the Communities of
S. Mary the Virgin, Wantage and S. Peter, Kilburn.

* A reduction allowed to Choirs.   Prepayment is necessary in all cases.

*The above prices include the postage. Copies can be obtained, upon application by
letter with remittance, from the Hon. Secretary—*

PERCY E. SANKEY, Esq., 44, RUSSELL SQUARE, LONDON, W.C.

The Society has arranged for instruction in the correct rendering of plainsong
to be given to Clergy, Organists and others, also for a Choirmaster to assist
Choirs adopting the music.   For particulars apply to the Hon. Secretary.

9 781087 925257